Green Finance and Investment

Energy Subsidy Reform in the Republic of Moldova

ENERGY AFFORDABILITY, FISCAL AND ENVIRONMENTAL IMPACTS

This work is published under the responsibility of the Secretary-General of the OECD. The opinions expressed and arguments employed herein do not necessarily reflect the official views of OECD member countries.

This document, as well as any data and any map included herein, are without prejudice to the status of or sovereignty over any territory, to the delimitation of international frontiers and boundaries and to the name of any territory, city or area.

Please cite this publication as:
OECD (2018), *Energy Subsidy Reform in the Republic of Moldova: Energy Affordability, Fiscal and Environmental Impacts*, Green Finance and Investment, OECD Publishing, Paris.
https://doi.org/10.1787/9789264292833-en

ISBN 978-92-64-29270-3 (print)
ISBN 978-92-64-29283-3 (PDF)

Series: Green Finance and Investment
ISSN 2409-0336 (print)
ISSN 2409-0344 (online)

The statistical data for Israel are supplied by and under the responsibility of the relevant Israeli authorities. The use of such data by the OECD is without prejudice to the status of the Golan Heights, East Jerusalem and Israeli settlements in the West Bank under the terms of international law.

Photo credits:
Cover © mika48/Shutterstock.com.

Corrigenda to OECD publications may be found on line at: www.oecd.org/about/publishing/corrigenda.htm.
© OECD 2018

You can copy, download or print OECD content for your own use, and you can include excerpts from OECD publications, databases and multimedia products in your own documents, presentations, blogs, websites and teaching materials, provided that suitable acknowledgment of the source and copyright owner(s) is given. All requests for public or commercial use and translation rights should be submitted to *rights@oecd.org*. Requests for permission to photocopy portions of this material for public or commercial use shall be addressed directly to the Copyright Clearance Center (CCC) at *info@copyright.com* or the Centre francais d'exploitation du droit de copie (CFC) at *contact@cfcopies.com*.

Foreword

This report presents the main findings and conclusions from an analysis of the social, fiscal and environmental consequences of reforming existing major energy subsidy schemes designed to support domestic users in the Republic of Moldova. The major subsidy measures include: i) a reduced value-added tax (VAT) rate on natural gas consumption; ii) VAT exemption on electricity; and iii) VAT exemption on heating. The study was carried out in response to a request addressed by the government of Moldova to the Organisation for Economic Co-operation and Development (OECD) to help conduct an energy affordability analysis.

This report is based on a methodology specifically designed for the analysis of energy affordability and a related computation model. These make it possible to assess the impact of a possible VAT increase on energy affordability for Moldovan households to consume adequate levels of natural gas, electricity and heat, as well as on greenhouse gas (GHG) emissions and on budgetary savings.

The current report was discussed with representatives of the government of Moldova on two occasions: in July 2017 and early March 2018, and reflects the feedback and comments provided by our partners in Moldova. We are particularly grateful to Lilia Palii, General State Secretary of the Republic of Moldova, for her lasting support for this work, as well as to Ina Crețu, Policy Advisor for the State Chancellery, who helped the OECD team throughout the project. Comments and suggestions from the Ministry of Economy and Infrastructure for improving the analysis were contributed by Calin Negură, Chief of Department for Energy Policy, and Denis Tumuruc, Deputy Chief of Department for Energy Policy, and were particularly appreciated by the project team.

The project was managed by Nelly Petkova (OECD). Rafal Stanek (SST-Consult, Poland) designed the analytical model and developed the analysis. This work would not have been possible without Mihai Roscovan (Business Consulting Institute, Moldova) who provided comprehensive background information, collected national level data and helped organise consultations with the government in Chisinau. Special thanks go to Krzysztof Michalak (OECD Environment Directorate) and Florens Flues (OECD Center for Tax Policy and Administration) for their constructive feedback on our research.

We are also grateful to Irina Belkahia (OECD) who provided overall administrative support to the project and to Olga Driga who translated the report into Romanian. The authors would like to thank Maria Dubois (OECD) for her help with formatting the report, Victoria Elliott who edited the report in English and Peter Vogelpoel who did the typesetting and the layout of the final manuscript. Janine Travers and Lupita Johanson of the OECD assisted with the processing of the publication.

The study was prepared within the framework of the "Greening Economies in the Eastern Neighbourhood" (EaP GREEN) Project, funded by the European Union and co-ordinated with the governments of the EaP countries. EaP GREEN has been implemented by the

OECD in partnership with United Nations (UN) partners: the UN Economic Commission for Europe (UNECE), UN Environment and UN Industrial Development Organization (UNIDO). The views expressed here are in no way intended to reflect the official opinion of the European Union.

Table of contents

Abbreviations and acronyms 9

Executive summary 11

Chapter 1. Moldova's energy subsidy reform: key analytical premises 13
    1.1. Major energy subsidy schemes in Moldova 14
    1.2. Energy intensity and GHG emissions 15
    1.3. Public debt 16
    Notes 18
    References 18

Chapter 2. Measuring energy poverty and ways to protect vulnerable groups in the European Union 19
    2.1. European Union practice 20
    2.2. Income and wealth inequality 20
    2.3. Defining vulnerable populations 22
    2.4. Types of measures to protect vulnerable groups used in the European Union 23
    2.5. Experience from neighbouring and transition countries 25
    Notes 26
    References 27

Chapter 3. Moldova's energy prices and energy affordability 29
    3.1. VAT policy for energy prices for households 30
    3.2. Electricity prices and affordability 30
    3.3. Natural gas for cooking 35
    3.4. Natural gas for cooking and heating 38
    3.5. Heating 39
    3.6. Combined use of electricity and natural gas for cooking and heating 40
    3.7. Conclusions 40
    Notes 42
    References 42

Chapter 4. Avoiding energy poverty in Moldova 45
    4.1. Overview of possible protection measures 46
    4.2. Identification of protection measures to be modelled and tested 47
    4.3. Main results of the modelling of the proposed protection measures 50
    4.4. Conclusions 53
    Notes 54
    References 54

Chapter 5. **Modelling the impacts of energy subsidy reform in Moldova** 55

    5.1. Introduction to the model and compensation scenarios analysed 56
    5.2. Results of the modelling 62
    Notes 80
    References 81

Chapter 6. **Conclusions and recommendations for Moldova** 83

    6.1. Major conclusions 84
    6.2. Selection of optimal social protection measures 84
    6.3. Main recommendations 88

Figures

Figure 2.1	Gini coefficient for selected EU member states, EECCA and USA	21
Figure 3.1	Electricity consumption for electric appliances and lighting in selected countries, kWh annually per household	31
Figure 3.2	Energy affordability for electricity: Share of spending on electricity in disposable household income and average annual spending on electricity, in EUR	33
Figure 3.3	Energy affordability for electricity, higher consumption: Share of spending on electricity in disposable household income and average annual spending on electricity, EUR	34
Figure 3.4	Energy affordability for natural gas: Share of spending on natural gas in disposable household income and average annual spending for natural gas, in EUR	37
Figure 3.5	Energy affordability for natural gas for cooking and heating: Share of spending on gas in disposable household income and average annual spending for natural gas, in EUR	38
Figure 3.6	Energy affordability for heating: Share of spending on heating in disposable household income and average annual spending for heating, in EUR	40
Figure 3.7	Energy affordability for the combined use of electricity and natural gas for cooking and heating: Share of spending on electricity and natural gas for cooking and heating in disposable household income, in EUR	41
Figure 5.1	Illustration of model algorithm	56
Figure 5.2	Illustration of a partial equilibrium model	57
Figure 5.3	Illustration of a price increase in a partial equilibrium model	57
Figure 5.4	Impact of subsidy reform in the electricity sector on end-user price, in MDL	63
Figure 5.5	Impact of subsidy reform in the electricity sector on GHG emissions for different scenarios, tCO_2 annually (VAT 20%)	64
Figure 5.6	Impact of subsidy reform in the electricity sector on public budget: budget income, expenditure and surplus for different scenarios, in MDL	66
Figure 5.7	Social impact of subsidy reform: percentage of spending on electricity in household disposable budgets for different scenarios, %	68
Figure 5.8	Impact of subsidy reform on end-user price for natural gas for cooking, in MDL	70
Figure 5.9	Impact of subsidy reform on end-user price for natural gas for cooking and heating, in MDL	70
Figure 5.10	Impact of subsidy reform in the gas sector on GHG emissions for different scenarios, tCO_2 annually	71
Figure 5.11	Impact of subsidy reform in the gas sector on the public budget – income, expenditure and surplus from the reform for different scenarios, in MDL	72
Figure 5.12	Social impact of subsidy reform: percentage of natural gas expenditure in disposable household income under different scenarios, %	74
Figure 5.13	Impact of subsidy reform on end-user price for heating, in MDL	74
Figure 5.14	Impact of subsidy reform in the heating sector on GHG emissions under different scenarios, tCO_2 annually	75
Figure 5.15	Impact of subsidy reform in the heating sector on the public budget: income, expenditure and surplus from the reform under different scenarios, in MDL	77
Figure 5.16	Social impact of subsidy reform: percentage of district heating expenditure in disposable household income under different scenarios, %	79

Tables

Table 1.1	Subsidy overview	14
Table 1.2	Energy intensity	15
Table 1.3	GHG emissions in Moldova, million tonnes per year	15
Table 1.4	Evolution of public sector debt, by component, 2014-16, MDL million	16
Table 1.5	Evolution of public sector debt, external vs. internal, 2014-16 in MDL million	17
Table 1.6	Evolution of public sector debt as a share of GDP, 2014-16, %	17
Table 3.1	Energy affordability for electricity, 2016	31
Table 3.2	Energy affordability for natural gas, 2016	35
Table 3.3	Energy affordability for heating, 2016	39
Table 4.1	Energy support programme, Chisinau, 2008-13	48
Table 4.2	Financial and investment measures	51
Table 5.1	Distribution of disposable household income per capita, %	59
Table 5.2	Average size of households, number of people	60
Table 5.3	Impact of subsidy reform in the electricity sector on GHG emissions under different scenarios, tCO_2 annually (VAT 20%)	64
Table 5.4	Impact of subsidy reform in the electricity sector on GHG emissions under different scenarios, tCO_2 annually (VAT 8%)	65
Table 5.5	Impact of subsidy reform in the electricity sector on GHG emissions under different scenarios, tCO_2 annually (VAT 5%)	65
Table 5.6	Impact of subsidy reform in the electricity sector on the public budget under different scenarios, in MDL annually (VAT 20%)	66
Table 5.7	Impact of subsidy reform in the electricity sector on the public budget under different scenarios, in MDL annually (VAT 8%)	67
Table 5.8	Impact of subsidy reform in the electricity sector on the public budget under different scenarios, in MDL annually (VAT 5%)	67
Table 5.9	Social impact of subsidy reform: percentage of electricity costs in disposable household income under different scenarios (VAT 20%)	68
Table 5.10	Social impact of subsidy reform: percentage of electricity costs in disposable household income under different scenarios (VAT 8%)	69
Table 5.11	Social impact of subsidy reform: percentage of electricity costs in disposable household income under different scenarios (VAT 5%)	69
Table 5.12	Impact of subsidy reform in the gas sector on GHG emissions under different scenarios, tCO_2 annually	71
Table 5.13	Impact of subsidy reform in the gas sector on the public budget under different scenarios, in MDL annually	72
Table 5.14	Social impact of subsidy reform: percentage of natural gas costs in household disposable income under different scenarios, %	73
Table 5.15	Impact of subsidy reform on the heating sector on GHG emissions under different scenarios, tCO_2 annually (VAT 20%)	75
Table 5.16	Impact of subsidy reform in the heating sector on GHG emissions under different scenarios, tCO_2 annually (VAT 8%)	76
Table 5.17	Impact of subsidy reform in the heating sector on GHG emissions under different scenarios, tCO_2 annually (VAT 5%)	76
Table 5.18	Impact of subsidy reform in the heating sector on the public budget under different scenarios, in MDL annually (VAT 20%)	77
Table 5.19	Impact of subsidy reform in the heating sector on the public budget under different scenarios, in MDL annually (VAT 8%)	78
Table 5.20	Impact of subsidy reform in the heating sector on the public budget under different scenarios, in MDL annually (VAT 5%)	78
Table 5.21	Social impact of subsidy reform: percentage of expenditures on heating in disposable household income under different scenarios, % (VAT 20%)	79
Table 5.22	Social impact of subsidy reform: percentage of expenditures on heating in disposable household income under different scenarios, % (VAT 8%)	80

Table 5.23	Social impact of subsidy reform: percentage of expenditures on heating in disposable household income under different scenarios, % (VAT 5%)	80
Table 6.1	Comparative assessment of social protection scenarios in the electricity sector	85
Table 6.2	Comparative assessment of VAT rate	86
Table 6.3	Comparative assessment of social protection scenarios in the natural gas sector	87

Boxes

Box 4.1	Overview of support programme in Chisinau	48
Box 5.1	Explanation of the partial equilibrium model	56

Abbreviations and acronyms

ANRE	National Agency for Energy Regulation
ATU	Administrative territorial unit
CA	Central Asia
CEER	Council of European Energy Regulators
DH	District heating
EaP	EU Eastern Partnership
EBRD	European Bank for Reconstruction and Development
EECCA	Eastern Europe, Caucasus and Central Asia
EHS	Environmentally harmful subsidy
EU	European Union
GDP	Gross domestic product
GHG	Greenhouse gas
HH	Household
IEA	International Energy Agency
LULUCF	Land use, land-use change and forestry
MDL	Moldovan leu
NBM	National Bank of Moldova
OECD	Organisation for Economic Co-operation and Development
PPP	Purchasing power parity
RM	Republic of Moldova
UK	United Kingdom of Great Britain
UNECE	United Nations Economic Commission for Europe
UNIDO	United Nations Industrial Development Organization
USA	United States of America
USD	US dollar
VAT	Value added tax
WTO	World Health Organization

Units of measurement

CO_2	Carbon dioxide
kg	Kilogramme
koe	Kilogramme of oil equivalent
ktoe	Kilotonne of oil equivalent
KW	Kilowatt
kWh	Kilowatt per hour
m^2	Square metre
m^3	Cubic metre
MW	Megawatt
MWh	Megawatt hour
t	Tonne
t/a	Tonnes annually
toe	Tonne of oil equivalent

Executive summary

Raising energy prices can make good economic and environmental sense but should not lead to increased affordability challenges when policy reform is viewed in its entirety. Using part of the additional revenue generated from higher taxes and putting in place well-designed social protection measures can help avoid the increased risk of energy affordability and even reduce it, if sufficient revenue is allocated to support vulnerable households.

An earlier analysis of energy subsidies in the European Union (EU) Eastern Partnership (EaP) countries conducted by the Organisation for Economic Co-operation and Development (OECD) in 2016-17 identified three large government support schemes that account for most of the fossil-fuel consumer subsidies in Moldova: i) the reduced value added tax (VAT) rate on natural gas consumption, ii) VAT exemption on electricity and iii) VAT exemption on heat consumption by domestic users. The standard VAT rate in Moldova is 20% but VAT for gas consumed by households is set at 8% and for electricity and heat consumption at 0%. The estimated revenue foregone by the government as a result of the reduced VAT rate on gas, electricity and heat consumption in 2015 alone amounted to USD 48.6 million.

The analysis in this study shows that reforming the VAT-related energy subsidies in Moldova, i.e. an increase of the VAT rate and a subsequent increase of the gas, electricity and heat tariffs for households, is worth implementing because the reform can yield significant budget revenue and a reduction (albeit modest) of greenhouse gas (GHG) emissions. However, given the significant impact of the VAT increase on consumer end-price and the related household spending on energy, the reform should not be introduced before a robust system of social protection measures is put in place.

Energy affordability is a key policy concern for Moldovan decision-makers. The analysis shows that the share of electricity costs in household income in Moldova is much higher (3.4%) than in other EU and South-Eastern European countries (e.g. 1.6% in Bulgaria, 2.6% in Romania, 0.7% in Slovenia) and some EaP countries (e.g. 2.2% in Ukraine). This situation is similar in the natural gas and heating sector as well.

The report analyses the VAT rate increase in terms of three main impacts: (i) change in the revenue stream to the public budget; (ii) costs that will need to be shouldered by the public budget to protect poor households affected by the VAT increase; and (iii) impact on household spending on energy.

The VAT increase is also modelled for three different VAT rates introduced in a step-wise manner: 5%, 8% and 20%, but most of the analysis is focused on the impact of the VAT rate increase up to 20% as required under Moldova's Association Agreement with the European Union. At the same time, the analysis shows that the main findings are consistent across all three VAT rate increases (5%, 8% and 20%) with respect to their social impact on end-user energy prices and environmental impact. The main difference observed concerns the impact on the budgetary surplus, which is obviously much higher under the 20% VAT increase scenario.

Experience from other countries shows that the easiest social protection measure to implement (administratively) is a voucher (certificate) system to compensate poor households for the increase in the VAT rate. The analysis presented in this report shows that this scenario has the lowest administrative costs (about USD 1.3 million under the 20% VAT scenario). Knowing the administrative cost of each protection measure is crucial, because the number of people who will need support if the reforms are implemented is significant, and this will have a direct impact on the budget.

Under the scenario of a 20% VAT increase, if a voucher system is introduced for gas, electricity and heat, the total cost for the public budget (the social transfer) is estimated to be about USD 47 million. The additional revenue that can be collected by the public budget due to the VAT rate increase is estimated to amount to about USD 77 million. The net budget surplus is significant and stands at about USD 30 million. The reform is also socially justifiable, as it is still better to protect poor households only rather than to maintain a subsidy that benefits all households, including those that are well off. In terms of environmental impact, especially with respect to GHG emissions, the analysis shows that under all scenarios, the impact is limited compared to the current level of emissions from the energy sector.

The results of the analysis show that raising the VAT rate for electricity consumption will be the easiest to roll out. This will have only a small impact on household electricity use and spending/income. On the other hand, increasing the VAT rate for heat consumption will significantly raise costs for households. Low-income groups (with income ranging from MLD 0 to MLD 1 000 per capita per month) will be hard hit by such an increase. If the VAT rate on heat is increased, the share of the heat consumption bill alone in household disposable income will increase by more than 20% for this income group.

The simulation results show that a reform that increases the VAT rate on electricity and gas can reduce energy affordability risk, if part of the additional revenues generated by the VAT increase is transferred back to households using an income-tested voucher transfer. In the case of both electricity and natural gas, the best social protection measure recommended in this study is "Income-tested, VAT compensation with voucher".

However, reforming the subsidy scheme for heat consumption is not recommended at this stage. First, increasing the price of heat (which is already very high in Moldova) as a result of the VAT rate increase may make end users switch from district heating (based on efficient co-generation of electricity and heat) to other energy sources that are less efficient. Second, most consumers do not have any instruments to measure and regulate the level of heating in their homes. This suggests that the higher price will not be an incentive for users to conserve heat since this will not lead to a decrease of their heat bills.

Implementing the reforms will not be easy and will require political will. To carry out these reform measures, Moldova will need to do more work to translate this analysis into actual legislative proposals. Any new fiscal policy package should include, among others, a clear definition of targeted low-income households and a carefully designed and resourced system to deliver support.

Chapter 1

Moldova's energy subsidy reform: key analytical premises

This chapter introduces and briefly discusses the major energy subsidy schemes in Moldova, the country's energy intensity and greenhouse gas (GHG) emissions and issues related to Moldova's public debt. These issues are of special importance, as they form part of the background information and data needed to assess the impact of energy subsidy reform.

Moldova is a net energy importer largely dependent on the Russian Federation (through Ukraine) for its natural gas supplies. This also determines the structure of its energy subsidies. Moldova does not have any large energy subsidy schemes. The main challenge in analysing its energy subsidies is the lack of transparency and publicly available information on the level of support for consumption and production of fossil fuels related to the status of the region of Transnistria.

1.1. Major energy subsidy schemes in Moldova

Earlier analysis of energy subsidies carried out by the OECD in 2016 and 2017 revealed that Moldova's energy sector has several schemes of government support. The analysis showed that most of the support goes to consumers. The three largest government support schemes, which account for most of the fossil-fuel consumer subsidies, are the reduced value added tax (VAT) rate on natural gas consumption and the VAT exemption on electricity and heat consumption by domestic users. The standard VAT rate in Moldova is 20%. VAT for gas consumed by households is set at 8% and for electricity and heat consumption at 0%. The estimated revenue foregone by the government as a result of the reduced VAT rate on gas, electricity and heat consumption in 2015 alone amounted to USD 48.6 million.

Table 1.1 summarises the main types of energy subsidies identified in previous research by subsidy type.

Table 1.1. **Subsidy overview**

Energy subsidy	Preliminary findings
Direct budget transfer of funds and liabilities	• Partially included in national subsidy definitions (except liabilities) • Compensation to households for high energy prices
Tax revenue foregone (the revenue that the government would receive if tax rates were higher)	• Not included in national subsidy definitions • No tax expenditure published by the government of Moldova • Reduced VAT rate for electricity (0%), heating (0%) and for natural gas (8%) for domestic users • Low gasoline and diesel excise tax rate • Exemption from environmental charges • Tax exemption for Moldovagaz (discontinued as of 2014)
Induced transfers (income or price support provided to producers or consumers through various regulations)	• Not included in the national subsidy definition • No price-gap estimates available from International Energy Agency or other international sources • Induced subsidy by not applying a proper tariff calculation and by failing to adjust tariffs for a long time
Transfer of risk	• Not included in the national subsidies definition • No significant discussion of the issue (except in terms of public investment in gas and electricity grids)

Source: OECD (2018).

Given their significance, this study analyses the reform of the energy subsidy schemes that result from the reduced VAT rate for electricity (0%), heating (0%) and for natural gas (8%) for domestic users.

1.2. Energy intensity and GHG emissions

Moldova's economy is both highly energy- and carbon-intensive. In 2013, its energy intensity stood at 427 kilogrammes of oil equivalent (koe) per EUR 1 000 or 139 koe per USD 1 000 purchasing power parity (PPP) adjusted (EC, 2015). This level is higher than the average energy intensity of the European Union (EU) countries, which, in 2014, stood at 121.7 koe per USD 1 000 (PPP adjusted) (Eurostat, 2016). Moldova's energy intensity in real prices is more than four times higher than the EU average, as illustrated in Table 1.2.

Table 1.2. **Energy intensity**

	2010	2011	2012	2013	2014	2015
Domestic consumption [ktoe]	2 209.0	2 237.0	2 145.0	2 160.0	2 319	2 350
Moldova GDP, EUR million	4 383	4 658	4 997	5054	4 799	4 226
Moldova energy intensity, toe/EUR 1 000	0.504	0.480	0.429	0.427	0.483	0.556
Energy intensity in EU, toe/EUR 1 000	0.1376	0.1303	0.1299	0.1282	0.1216	0.1204
Ratio of Moldova/EU energy intensity	3.66	3.69	3.30	3.33	3.97	4.62

Source: Climate Change Office. Republic of Moldova. www.clima.md. Accessed in September 2017.

Moldova's carbon intensity (measured in kilogrammes of CO_2 from energy use per USD of GDP) has significantly declined, from 4.4 in the early 1990s to 1.9 kg CO_2 per real GDP in 2013 (2010 USD, without Land Use, Land-Use Change and Forestry (LULUCF).[1] And yet, its carbon intensity is higher, even when compared to most other countries in Eastern Europe, Caucasus and Central Asia (IEA, 2016).

Table 1.3. **GHG emissions in Moldova, million tonnes per year**

	1990	2000	2010	2011	2012	2013	2014	2015
CO_2 without LULUCF	34.8952	6.4504	9.6570	9.8288	9.5065	8.4882	9.2609	9.3956
CO_2 with LULUCF	29.0128	0.3199	6.3596	7.1157	6.4892	5.8716	6.5376	6.4910
Aggregated emissions (CO_2 equivalents)	43.4000	11.2078	14.2635	14.5031	13.7486	11.4349	14.1995	13.9533
Net emissions (LULUCF)	-5.8197	-6.0570	-3.2301	-2.6440	-2.9451	-2.5470	-2.6610	-2.8454
Aggregated emissions including emissions/removals from LULUCF (CO_2 equivalents)	37.5804	5.1507	11.0334	11.8591	10.8034	8.8878	11.5384	11.1079

Source: Climate Change Office. Republic of Moldova. www.clima.md. Accessed in September 2017.

The IEA estimates that the per capita CO_2 emissions from fossil-fuel burning in 2015 in Moldova were 2.12 tonnes. For 2011, the EBRD The Low Carbon Transition report estimates 2 tonnes of CO_2 per capita per year as a sustainable emission target (EBRD, 2011). While Moldova is close to this target, addressing the high levels of energy and carbon intensity of the economy requires urgent measures.

1.3. Public debt

The following section is based on the Ministry of Finance public report for 2016 (MoF, 2017).[2]

In 2016, the public sector debt balance increased by MDL 16 102.6 million or by 37.2% as compared to the end of 2015, and amounted to MDL 59 371.9 million. According to data on the GDP for the year 2016, the share of public sector debt in GDP, as of 31 December 2016, stood at 37.8%, e.g. 8.8 percentage points more than the share at the end of 2015.

Table 1.4. **Evolution of public sector debt, by component, 2014-16, MDL million**

Nominal value, MDL million	31 Dec. 2014[a]	31 Dec. 2015	31 Dec. 2016
State debt	27 470.6	33 509.2	50 785.8
Debt NBM (National Bank of Moldova)	6 100.6	6 669.7	5 839.9
Debt companies from public sector[b]	2 544.9	2 673.4	2 339.2
Local government debt[c]	286.0	416.8	406.9
Total	36 402.2	43 269.2	59 371.9

Notes: a. The public sector debt balance as of 31 December 2014 was updated in 2016 as a result of additional information provided by some public sector enterprises.

b. Includes debt directly contracted by public sector enterprises with maturity equal to or higher than 1 year.

c. Includes debt directly contracted by administrative territorial units (ATU) with maturity equal to or higher than 1 year.

Source: National Bureau of Statistics of Moldova. www.statistica.md/index.php?l=en. Accessed in September 2017.

The increase in the public sector debt balance at the end of 2016 compared to the end of 2015 is conditioned by the increase of the state debt balance by MDL 17 276.6 million. In the same period, the other components of the public sector debt decreased. Respectively, the balance of the National Bank of Moldova (NBM) debt decreased by MDL 829.8 million, the debt of the public sector enterprises decreased by MDL 334.2 million, and the administrative territorial unit (ATU)[3] debt, which decreased by MDL 10.0 million.

On 31 December 2016, the external debt of the public sector amounted to USD 1 778.9 million (the equivalent of MDL 35 544.7 million), or 59.9% of the total public sector debt, and the domestic debt of the public sector constituted MDL 23 827.2 million (40.1%). In 2016, the public sector debt increased and was mainly influenced by the domestic debt of the public sector, which registered an upward trend of approximately 143.0%.

Arrears on the loans of the public sector entities were recorded, as of 31 December 2016, in the amount of MDL 299.7 million, made up entirely of arrears on the internal loans of the public sector and the enterprises of ATUs. Compared to the end of 2015, the value of arrears on domestic loans increased by MDL 67.9 million or 29.3%, and compared to the same period of 2014, it increased by 10.9%. Arrears to external public sector loans were not recorded.

At the end of 2015, the state debt amounted to MDL 50 785.8 million, increasing by MDL 17 276.6 million or by 51.6%, influenced especially by an increase of the domestic state debt by MDL 14 294.2 million and of the external state debt by MDL 2 982.4 million, respectively.

Table 1.5. **Evolution of public sector debt, external vs. internal, 2014-16 in MDL million**

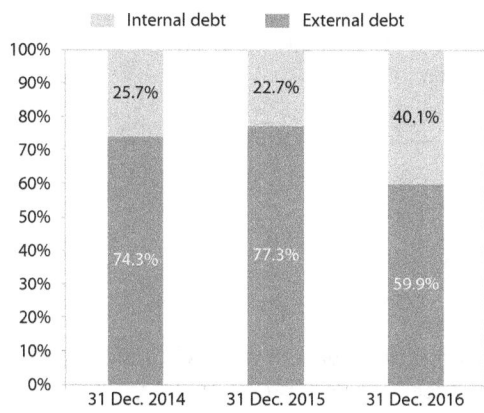

Nominal value	31 Dec. 2014	31 Dec. 2015	31 Dec. 2016
External debt	27 029.6	33 459.1	35 544.7
Internal debt	9 372.6	9 810.1	23 827.2
Total	**36 402.2**	**43 269.2**	**59 371.9**

Source: National Bureau of Statistics of Moldova. National Bureau of Statistics of Moldova. www.statistica.md/index.php?l=en. Accessed in September 2017.

The 2016 GDP data show that the percentage of government debt in GDP, as of 31 December 2016, was 37.8%, increasing by 10.4 percentage points compared with the end of 2015.

In 2016, there was an increase of the share of domestic debt in GDP, which at the end of 2016 constituted 16.0%, increasing by 10.1 percentage points compared to the same period of 2015, and by 9.7 percentage points compared to the end of 2014. This increase is explained by the issue, in October 2016, of government securities in the amount of MDL 13 341.2 million for the Ministry of Finance, to execute the payment obligations derived from state guarantees granted to the National Bank of Moldova to guarantee emergency loans.

Table 1.6. **Evolution of public sector debt as a share of GDP, 2014-16, %**

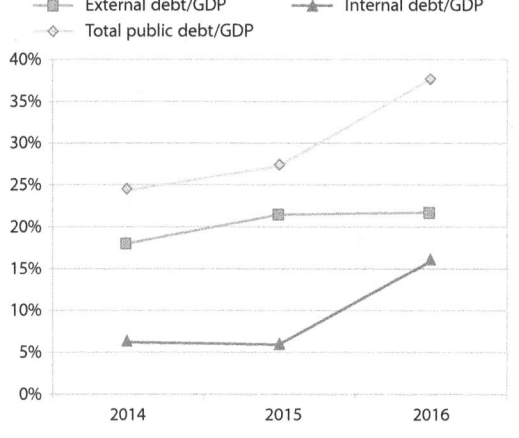

Nominal values MDL million	31 Dec. 2014	31 Dec. 2015	31 Dec. 2016
External debt/GDP	18.2%	21.4%*	21.8%
Internal debt/GDP	6.3%	5.9%	16.0%
Total public debt/GDP	24.5%	27.3%*	37.8%
GDP (MDL million)	112 049.6	122 563.0*	134 476.0

*Final GDP for 2015.

Source: National Bureau of Statistics of Moldova. www.statistica.md/index.php?l=en. Accessed in September 2017.

Notes

1. GoM (2015).
2. www.mf.gov.md/files/files/Datoria%20de%20Stat/raport%20dat%20publ/Raport%202016.pdf.
3. ATU is a collective term for all administrative organisational units in the territories (below national level). In Moldova, these include the first level – villages, cities and towns – and the second level – *rayons* (32), Chisinau, Balti and Bender municipalities. It also includes two autonomous territorial units: Gagauzia and Transnistria.

References

Climate Change Office of Moldova (2017), *GHG Emissions of Moldova*, Climate Change Office of Moldova, Chisinau. www.clima.md. Accessed in September 2017.

EBRD (2011), *The Low Carbon Transition*, European Bank for Reconstruction and Development, London.

EC (2015), *Communication from the Commission to the European Parliament, the Council, the European Economic and Social Committee, and the Committee of the Regions and the European Investment Bank: A Framework Strategy for a Resilient Energy Union with a Forward-Looking Climate Change Policy*, COM(2015) 80 final, European Commission, Brussels. http://eur-lex.europa.eu/resource.html?uri=cellar:1bd46c90-bdd4-11e4-bbe1-01aa75ed71a1.0001.03/DOC_1&format=PDF.

Eurostat (2016), *Energy Intensity of the Economy, kg of oil equivalent per 1 000 EUR, Eurostat*, Brussels. http://ec.europa.eu/eurostat/tgm/table.do?tab=table&init=1&language=en&pcode=tsdec360&plugin=1.

GoM (2015), *Republic of Moldova's Intended National Determined Contribution*, Government of the Republic of Moldova, Chisinau.

IEA (2016), *World Energy Statistics and Balances*, online data service 2017 Edition, Organisation for Economic Co-operation and Development/International Energy Agency, Paris. https://www.iea.org/statistics/relateddatabases/worldenergystatisticsandbalances/.

MoF (2017), *Raport privind situația în domeniul datoriei sectorului public, garanțiilor de stat și recreditării de stat pe anul 2016* (Report on public sector debt, state guarantees and state re-crediting for 2016), Ministry of Finance of the Republic of Moldova, Chisinau. http://mf.gov.md/sites/default/files/raport_pe_anul_2016.pdf.

NBS (2017), *Public Sector Debt*, National Bureau of Statistics of Moldova, Chisinau. www.statistica.md/index.php?l=en. Accessed in September 2017.

OECD (2018), *Inventory of Energy Subsidies in the EU's Eastern Partnership Countries*, Green Finance and Investment, OECD Publishing, Paris, https://doi.org/10.1787/9789264284319-en.

Chapter 2

Measuring energy poverty and ways to protect vulnerable groups in the European Union

> *This chapter introduces the definition of energy and fuel poverty on the basis of the experience of different European Union member states. It also briefly discusses several major types of measures that European Union countries use to protect vulnerable groups at risk of energy poverty.*

2.1. European Union practice

There are two key European Union (EU) Directives that provide the framework to identify vulnerable consumers and address this vulnerability. These are the Directives concerning the common rules for the internal market in natural gas (2009/73/EC)[1] and electricity (2009/72/EC).[2]

For electricity, Article 3 (points 7 and 8) states that:[3]

"Member States shall take appropriate measures to protect final customers, and shall, in particular, ensure that there are adequate safeguards to protect vulnerable customers. In this context, each Member State shall define the concept of vulnerable customers which may refer to energy poverty and, inter alia, to the prohibition of disconnection of electricity to such customers in critical times. Member States shall ensure that rights and obligations linked to vulnerable customers are applied. In particular, they shall take measures to protect final customers in remote areas…"

Furthermore, the number of European Union member states that have included the concept of vulnerable customers in energy or other relevant laws has increased from 8 in 2009 to 17 in 2013 (VCWG, 2013). Vulnerable consumers are usually defined in terms of energy affordability. Several types of criteria are used to classify consumers as vulnerable to the risk of having problems paying their energy bills. These include:

- income thresholds (for example, as in Greece, Malta and Romania)
- share of income required to meet adequate fuel requirements (as in the United Kingdom)
- consumer characteristics, for example, age, illness, etc. (as in Belgium, Romania, Slovenia and Spain, as well as for winter and cold weather payments in the United Kingdom).

An Energy Union Communication from 2015 begins the discussion on vulnerable consumers with energy poverty whose causes it sees as "a combination of low-income and general poverty conditions, inefficient homes and a housing tenure system that fails to encourage energy efficiency". According to the Communication, protecting vulnerable consumers is the primary means of reducing energy poverty:

"When phasing out regulated prices, Member States need to propose a mechanism to protect vulnerable consumers, which could preferably be provided through the general welfare system. If provided through the energy market, it could be implemented through schemes such as a solidarity tariff or as a discount on energy bills. The cost of such schemes needs to be covered by non-eligible consumers collectively. Hence, it is important that such a system is well targeted to keep overall costs low and to limit the distortions deriving from regulated prices (e.g. not increase further tariff deficits in Member States)".[4]

2.2. Income and wealth inequality

Income or wealth distribution across residents is usually measured by the Gini coefficient. The Gini coefficient, developed by the Italian statistician and sociologist Corrado Gini in 1912, measures inequality in a group or across levels of income. The Gini coefficient is measured on a scale between 0 and 1 (or 0% and 100%). A measure of 0 implies complete equality (everyone gets the same income) and 100 is perfect inequality (one person gets all of the income). A lower Gini coefficient implies a more equal distribution of income. The world income Gini coefficient is relatively high, due mainly to high inequality, particularly among the large populations of the BRIC (Brazil, the Russian Federation, India, China) countries. In Europe and the counties of Eastern Europe, Caucasus and Central Asia (EECCA), the Gini coefficients are lower.

Moldova, with a Gini coefficient of 27% in 2015, is among the countries with the lowest inequality. Figure 2.1 shows the Gini coefficients for selected EU member states, EECCA countries and the United States.

Figure 2.1. **Gini coefficient for selected EU member states, EECCA and USA**

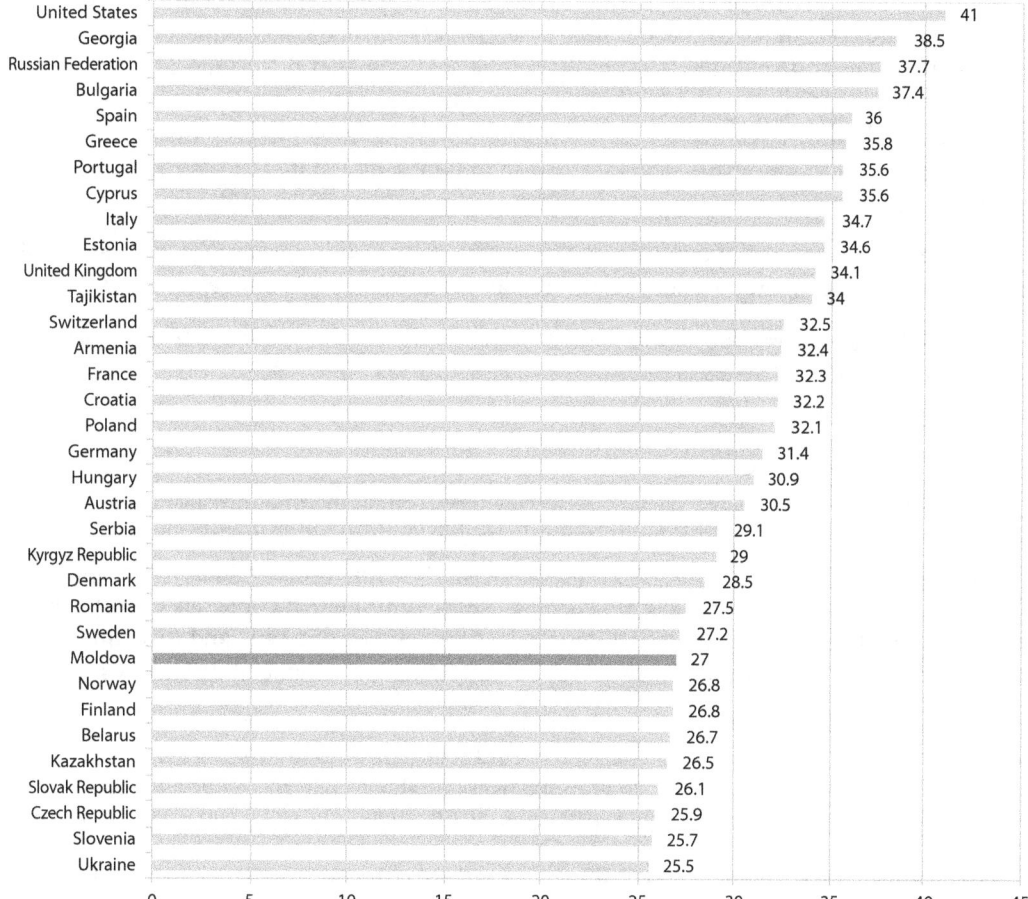

Source: World Bank (2018), World Bank database, https://data.worldbank.org/indicator/SI.POV.GINI/?end=2015&start=2015&type=shaded&view=bar. Accessed on 15 March 2018.

Moldova's low inequality implies that the impact of the energy subsidy reform will be relatively evenly distributed across the various income groups. This, however, does not mean that many of these groups do not qualify as vulnerable customers. Current legislation in Moldova does not provide specific definitions of energy poverty or vulnerable consumers.

Defining vulnerable populations in the European Union member states is discussed in the next section of this chapter.

2.3. Defining vulnerable populations

In the European Union, the populations at risk of poverty are defined as households with an income of 60% of the median national income. The primary drivers of energy poverty in Europe are identified as a combination of low income levels, high energy prices and low energy-efficiency levels (in particular in buildings). In 2012, of the EU member states, Romania was found to be most at risk of poverty (40%-50% of the population). In this context, Romania could thus be used as a basis for comparison and as a proxy for analysing the case of the Republic of Moldova.

As for energy and fuel poverty, the EU member states use various definitions. In general, these definitions are focused on *income thresholds*, below which households are considered at risk of energy/fuel poverty, and *energy expenditure thresholds*, above which households are considered at risk of energy/fuel poverty. The most common measure used is the percentage of disposable household income spent on energy services; typically, this rate is 10%.[5] In addition, in the United Kingdom, the use of target comfort levels defined by the World Health Organization (WHO) is a type of relative poverty line defining the minimum consumption levels necessary to maintain social status. These indicators are reviewed below.

For the purposes of the analysis of this study, we use the **percentage of disposable household income spent on energy services as the measure of energy affordability**.

The analysis in the rest of this chapter and the discussion of the definitions in the individual EU member states is based on Pye et al. (2015).

EU countries' definitions

In **Austria**, households are defined as at risk based on an income threshold below which the household is considered to be at risk of energy poverty, taken with an expenditure threshold. The expenditure threshold is based on the low-income household spending a higher than average percentage of its disposable household income on energy. Other indicators are also considered, including information on past due bills and disconnections, as well as subjective indicators, such as permanent household financial difficulties.

In **Cyprus**,[6] households are considered to be in energy poverty based on factors including low income (based on income tax returns), professional status, marital status and specific health conditions that may make users unable to pay the costs for a reasonable electricity supply, given that these costs represent a high percentage of disposable income.

In **France**, while no quantitative threshold is used, energy poverty is deemed to occur when a person has difficulties having enough energy supply to satisfy elementary needs, due either to insufficient resources (low income) or inadequate housing conditions.

In **Italy**, according to the definition proposed by the national regulator, households are defined as vulnerable when they spend more than 5% of disposable income on electricity and 10% on gas.

In the **Republic of Ireland**, energy poverty is associated with households that cannot attain an acceptable level of energy services (heating, lighting, gas, etc.) due to affordability concerns. According to official definitions, energy poverty is defined as spending more than 10% of disposable household income on energy services.

In **Slovakia**, a proposal was made under which energy poverty would be associated with average monthly household expenditures on electricity, gas and heat exceeding a certain share of average monthly household income. The threshold is set based on national statistics.

England defines a fuel-poor household as one with residual income (after fuel costs) below the poverty line and with energy costs higher than the median for a typical household of the type in question. England also continues to report the 10% threshold for purposes of comparison, defining a "fuel-poor" household as one that needs to spend more than 10% of its income on all fuel use to heat its home to an adequate standard of warmth (21°C in the living room and 18°C in other rooms, as per WHO recommendations). Thus, in England, not only do expenditures influence the definition of households that are risk, but also the standard level of warmth.

In **Northern Ireland**, a household is considered to be in fuel poverty if it has to spend more than 10% of its income on household fuel use to maintain an acceptable level of temperature in the home. This is analogous to the WHO "satisfactory heating regime" recommendations.

Scotland defines fuel poverty as spending more than 10% of income (including housing benefits) on all household fuel use in order to maintain a "satisfactory heating regime", which is defined as 23°C in the living room and 18°C in other rooms, maintained for 16 hours in every 24-hour period for households with older persons, persons with chronic illnesses, or disabled persons and 21°C and 18°C for nine hours in every 24-hour period in other households (16 out of 24 hours on weekends).

Wales defines fuel poverty as spending more than 10% of income (including housing benefits) on all household fuel use, to maintain a "satisfactory heating regime", as defined in Scotland. The regulations also provide for a definition of extreme fuel poverty if household spending reaches more than 20% of all income.

In addition, in the United Kingdom as a whole, winter and cold weather benefits are paid to certain demographic groups (for example, old age pensioners, the disabled, etc.) regardless of income. To qualify, beneficiaries must be residents of the area from which they apply on a given reference date in the autumn.

Energy poverty can be also defined as an inability to maintain a satisfactory level of household temperature. The percentage of households that are not adequately heated varies across European countries, but is generally significant. Statistics for 2013 show that over 30% of the people of Turkey, Bulgaria and Lithuania lived in energy poverty. In Italy and Greece, this percentage was over 20%.

2.4. Types of measures to protect vulnerable groups used in the European Union

In the EU member states, a measure designed to protect vulnerable consumers and address energy poverty explicitly provides additional consumer protection to vulnerable groups and has some targeted aspect to improve the building envelope (to reduce energy use), provide additional information or support, or offer financial relief in the payment of energy bills.

Certain supporting measures also used do not explicitly target consumers but support other targeted measures. Examples include improving energy use in social housing, improving access to information on tariffs, social welfare support and protection against being disconnected.

The types of targeted measures used in the EU can be divided into four groups:

1. **Financial support:** These include support for paying bills. Such measures are usually focused on short-term relief.
2. **Investment support:** These include measures and programmes intended to improve the energy efficiency of the building stock and home appliances.
3. **Consumer protection:** These measures protect consumers on the retail market, for example, by protecting vulnerable customers from being disconnected.
4. **Raising public awareness:** These measures are aimed at improving the understanding of consumer rights and information on market tariffs and energy-saving measures.

A study of over 280 measures was conducted across all EU member states (Pye et al., 2015). Of these, 40% were identified as being specifically targeted at vulnerable consumers or those in or at risk of energy poverty.[7]

Financial measures

Over 40% of the EU member states use financial intervention measures as the primary tool for supporting vulnerable customers.[8] The intent is to provide cost relief, rather than to address the underlying problem of why some groups cannot afford energy costs. The types of measures used are as follows (the number in the brackets shows the percentage application of the given type of measure as a sub-set of financial measures):

- social support – for housing and energy costs (36%) – transferred as general welfare payments
- energy cost subsidies and payments (32%) – payments earmarked for energy costs;
- energy cost subsidies and payments, for elderly customers (7%)
- social tariffs (20%) – this is a tariff set specifically for vulnerable customers. This, of course, requires defining a vulnerable customer. It could mean, for example, a customer who is already part of a poverty support programme, a disabled person, an elderly person or a person living in social housing with gas heating
- negotiated tariffs with an energy utility (5%).[9]

One of the key challenges of providing such support is whether the financial assistance should be targeted or whether the policy should be applied using a blanket approach (for example, providing support to all users below a certain income threshold). Financial assistance entails a significant administrative burden, whilst the blanket approach risks providing support to customers who do not actually need it.

If general welfare payments are based on a basic consumption bundle considered necessary for normal life, expenditures on energy will be included in such a bundle. If energy prices increase, the price of the consumption bundle will increase, and hence welfare payments will increase. In this case, there is an automatic adjustment for energy price increases. If the general welfare system works well (i.e. supports poor households in need of support) no additional measure would be necessary for energy affordability. Integrating support for higher energy prices in the general welfare system would reduce the need for a new system for a cash transfer or for issuing vouchers, and should lower administrative costs significantly. Germany is one such example, where rising electricity prices (with an increase of roughly 100% in the last 15 years) have hardly been an issue, because the higher electricity prices automatically trigger higher welfare payments.

Energy-efficiency programmes

All EU member states implement some kind of energy-efficiency measures, although typically they are not always targeted at vulnerable consumers or low-income households at risk of energy poverty. The types of measures include:

- grants, loans or tax incentives for retrofits, non-targeted (42% of those reviewed)
- grants, loans or tax incentives for retrofits, targeted at vulnerable consumers (21% of those reviewed)
- grants, non-targeted (8%) and targeted (4%), for replacement of appliances
- energy-efficiency improvements for rental property (% unspecified)
- energy-efficiency improvements of social housing (8%)
- advice on energy efficiency (6%), including support for energy audits.[10]

Additional consumer protection

Among EU member states, 40% use disconnection safeguards as the primary measure for protecting vulnerable customers.

Information and awareness campaigns

Measures of this kind include the organisation of national, municipal and local advice centres, promoting transparent billing, smart metering, energy-efficiency certification of buildings, and price comparisons.

2.5. Experience from neighbouring and transition countries

In **Ukraine**, the ongoing reforms provide an interesting case for the Republic of Moldova. In Ukraine, energy-efficiency reforms are planned to go through a transition toward "subsidy monetisation". When fully implemented, under this scheme the customer would be able to choose how to spend the support received, for example, by paying energy costs, investing in energy-efficiency improvements, or both. This requires many preconditions, including heating, electricity and fuel sector reforms, development and testing of necessary infrastructure (accounts and processing centres), financial recovery of the district heating sector (adequate payment discipline and collections), creation and verification of a single database of subsidy recipients, and sustainable liquidity level required in the State Budget so that delays in settlements do not occur.

Armenia's power sector reform is typically considered a success story. The core elements of the reform were a gradual transition to cost-based tariffs, the unbundling of a part of the state-owned, vertically integrated utility and the introduction of a new regulatory framework. The reforms eventually brought nearly a 100% collection rate on sales, with only 4% commercial losses. Tariffs are moving toward full-cost recovery levels. Service has improved and has essentially not been interrupted. Significantly, the government of Armenia has unburdened itself of fiscal and quasi-fiscal support to the power sector. Early in the process, in the late 1990s, the increase in tariffs led some 80% of households surveyed to switch to cheaper, often dirtier fuel sources. For example, 60% of households substituted wood fuel and 24% natural gas for electric heating. In 1999, Armenia introduced a family benefit programme that provides cash payments to poor households. By 2006, the support was available to only 18% of households, even though the income of nearly 43% of households fell below the poverty line. In addition, the social transfers were insufficient to make much of an impact on heating costs.[11] This situation has steadily improved over time. This example illustrates the need to work consistently towards sector reforms whilst optimising social support, to ensure that the costs of the reforms do not significantly affect lower income groups.

Notes

1. The European Parliament and the Council of the European Union (2009a).

2. The European Parliament and the Council of the European Union (2009b).

3. For natural gas, the same provision is found in the European Parliament and the Council of the European Union (2009a) under Article 3 (points 3 and 4).

4. EC (2015), p.12.

5. Disposable household income has several possible definitions. The most important are: household income after tax; and household income after tax net of social benefits. For the best possible analysis of potential social impacts of support programmes for vulnerable consumers, disposable household income should be divided into various income groups, such as by deciles, quintiles or quartiles, as well as reported as mean and median for each of these groups. These data are not always available, however, as is the case in the Republic of Moldova, where household income data are reported by region, with a separate distinction for the cities of Chisinau and Balti. In the Republic of Moldova, disposable household income is particularly difficult to measure, as a recent national survey emphasises. In this survey, respondents listed as basic sources of livelihood: salary or income of enterprise or family farm (35%), salary or income of some members of my family (45%), sale of products of part-time farm (9%), use of products of part-time farm (41%), social benefits (42%) and assistance from friends and relatives (10%) (CISR, 2017).

6. Note by Turkey: The information in this document with reference to "Cyprus" relates to the southern part of the Island. There is no single authority representing both Turkish and Greek Cypriot people on the Island. Turkey recognises the Turkish Republic of Northern Cyprus (TRNC). Until a lasting and equitable solution is found within the context of the United Nations, Turkey shall preserve its position concerning the "Cyprus issue".

   Note by all the European Union Member States of the OECD and the European Union: The Republic of Cyprus is recognised by all members of the United Nations with the exception of Turkey. The information in this document relates to the area under the effective control of the Government of the Republic of Cyprus.

7. Pye, S. et al. (2015).

8. Pye, S. et al. (2015), op. cit.

9. Ibid.

10. Ibid.

11. Sargsyan, G. et al. (2006).

References

CISR (2017), *Public Opinion Survey: Residents of Moldova, September-October 2017*, Center for Insights in Survey Research, www.iri.org/sites/default/files/wysiwyg/2017-11-8_moldova_poll_presentation.pdf.

CEER (2012), *CEER Status Review of Customer and Retail Market Provisions from the 3rd Package as of 1 January 2012*, Council of European Energy Regulators. Ref: C12-CEM-55-04, November, Brussels, https://www.ceer.eu/documents/104400/-/-/f82e3e15-db9d-1017-7b20-c787da279bd7.

EC (2015), *Communication from the Commission to the European Parliament, the Council, the European Economic and Social Committee, and the Committee of the Regions and the European Investment Bank – A Framework Strategy for a Resilient Energy Union with a Forward-Looking Climate Change Policy*, COM(2015) 80 final, European Commission, Brussels, http://eur-lex.europa.eu/resource.html?uri=cellar:1bd46c90-bdd4-11e4-bbe1-01aa75ed71a1.0001.03/DOC_1&format=PDF.

Flues, F. and K. Van Dender (2017), *The Impact of Energy Taxes on the Affordability of Domestic Energy*, OECD Taxation Working Papers, No. 30, OECD Publishing, Paris, http://dx.doi.org/10.1787/08705547-en.

Pye, S. et al. (2015), *Energy Poverty and Vulnerable Consumers in the Energy Sector across the EU: Analysis of Policies and Measures*, Insight_E, https://ec.europa.eu/energy/sites/ener/files/documents/INSIGHT_E_Energy%20Poverty%20-%20Main%20Report_FINAL.pdf.

Sargsyan, G. et al. (2006), *From Crisis to Stability in the Armenian Power Sector. Lessons Learned from Armenia's Energy Reform Experience*, World Bank, Washington, DC, http://siteresources.worldbank.org/INTARMENIA/Resources/Armenia-power-sector-reform.pdf.

The European Parliament and the Council of the European Union (2009a), *Directive 2009/73/EC of the European Parliament and of the Council of 13 July 2009 Concerning Common Rules for the Internal Market in Natural Gas and Repealing Directive 2003/55/EC*, Official Journal of the European Union, http://eur-lex.europa.eu/LexUriServ/LexUriServ.do?uri=OJ:L:2009:211:0094:0136:en:PDF.

The European Parliament and the Council of the European Union (2009b), *Directive 2009/72/EC of the European Parliament and of the Council of 13 July 2009 Concerning Common Rules for the Internal Market in Electricity and Repealing Directive 2003/54/EC*, Official Journal of the European Union, http://eur-lex.europa.eu/legal-content/EN/TXT/PDF/?uri=CELEX:32009L0072&from=EN.

VCWG (2013), *Guidance Document on Vulnerable Consumers*, November 2013, Vulnerable Consumer Working Group. https://ec.europa.eu/energy/sites/ener/files/documents/20140106_vulnerable_consumer_report_0.pdf.

World Bank (2018), *World Bank Database: Gini Index*, World Bank, Washington, DC. https://data.worldbank.org/indicator/SI.POV.GINI/?end=2015&start=2015&type=shaded&view=bar. Accessed on 15 March 2018.

Chapter 3

Moldova's energy prices and energy affordability

This chapter looks at energy prices for electricity, natural gas and heating in Moldova and analyses how affordable it is for households to consume energy. To define energy affordability, average annual energy costs are compared to average annual household income. To provide a better sense of where Moldova stands in relation to other countries, energy affordability is reviewed in a selected number of countries of the European Union (EU), South East Europe, EU Eastern Partnership and the Central Asia region.

To define energy affordability, we compare average annual energy costs with average annual household income. The average annual energy costs depend on energy prices and the consumption of the particular energy carrier. Retail energy prices are affected by many factors (e.g. price of fossil fuels, transmission and distribution costs, etc.). Most countries impose value added tax (VAT) and excise tax on both natural gas and electricity, which further increases energy prices. This issue is of particular importance in this analysis, given that reduced VAT rates on energy carriers are a major subsidy scheme in many countries, including in the Republic of Moldova.

Actual energy consumption levels also depend on factors including:
- income of the population (higher income will result in higher consumption)
- energy prices (higher energy prices lead to lower consumption)
- energy efficiency (better insulation leads to lower consumption)
- billing methods (volumetric billing, especially billing on a monthly basis, may encourage households to save energy)
- type of energy used
- climate conditions.

When analysing Moldova's energy prices and energy affordability, it is also important to compare Moldova with other countries, since this can give a better sense of where the country stands. Energy affordability will be considered in a selected number of countries of the European Union (EU), South East Europe, EU Eastern Partnership (EaP) and Central Asia (CA). Given the complexity of consumption levels and to facilitate comparison, the same consumption level is used for all countries in the analysis.

3.1. VAT policy for energy prices for households

The EU member states set value added tax (VAT) and excise tax on both electricity and natural gas. Most EU countries use their maximum VAT rates for electricity. The exceptions are Ireland (13.5%), Greece (13%), France (5.5%), Italy (10%), Luxembourg (8%), Malta (5%) and the United Kingdom (UK) (5%). Most of these countries set the same lower VAT rate on heating, except for Malta, Italy and the UK, which set higher rates. In addition, for VAT on heating, Latvia sets a lower rate at 12%, Lithuania at 9%, and Hungary at 5%. As for natural gas, the EU countries that set reduced VAT rates are Ireland, Greece, France, Italy, Latvia, Malta and the UK[1] (EC, 2017).

From non-EU countries, Serbia imposes a reduced, 10%, VAT rate on natural gas and heating and the Kyrgyz Republic imposes a 0% VAT rate[2] on gas and heating.

3.2. Electricity prices and affordability

This analysis covers 44 countries, all EU members and a selected number of countries of South-Eastern Europe. Of the EaP and CA countries, detailed data for this comparative overview were available only for Armenia, Georgia, Moldova, Ukraine and the Kyrgyz Republic. The electricity prices in this sample vary from EUR 0.01 per kWh in the Kyrgyz Republic to EUR 0.30 per kWh in Denmark.

Electricity prices in Moldova for household consumers are similar to those in Bosnia and Herzegovina, Bulgaria and Montenegro. The electricity prices for household consumers in most of the EaP and CA countries and Serbia are lower than the prices in Moldova. The electricity prices for household consumers in the new EU member states are only slightly higher than those in Moldova, while these prices are significantly higher in all other EU countries, particularly in those that have developed feed-in tariffs, such as Germany or Denmark.

The electricity price, however, does not provide any information on energy affordability for consumers. To define energy affordability with respect to electricity consumption, it is necessary to calculate the average annual cost of electricity consumption of the average household (average annual consumption x average electricity price) and compare it with the average annual household income.

According to the Energy Strategy of the Republic of Moldova until 2030 (GoM, 2013), in 2016, the average annual consumption of electricity is 1 277 kWh per person. In wealthier countries, the annual electricity consumption of households is expected to be higher, but for the sake of comparison, this analysis uses the same consumption level across all countries. In some countries, electricity is also used for heating or cooling and then the average consumption is higher. For comparison, Figure 3.1 shows the average consumption of electricity for electric appliances and lighting.

Figure 3.1. **Electricity consumption for electric appliances and lighting in selected countries, kWh annually per household**

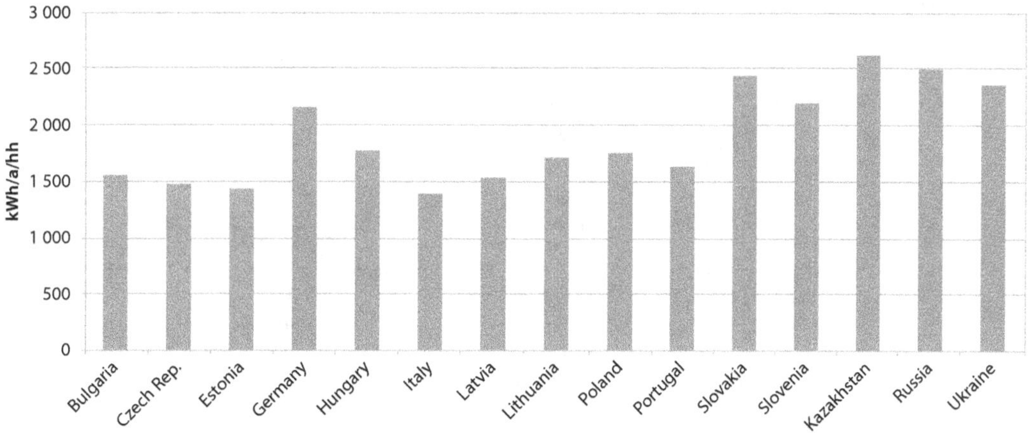

Source: World Energy Council, Energy efficiency indicators database. https://www.worldenergy.org/data/efficiency-indicators/. Accessed on 10 June 2017.

Taking into account the average annual income, the least expensive countries are shown to be Norway and Liechtenstein, where average annual energy costs account for only 0.23% and 0.24% of disposable household income, respectively. In most of the countries, energy costs account for 1%-2% of household disposable income. Moldova, at 3.39%, and Romania, at 2.56%, are the two countries in the dataset whose population spends the most of its disposable income on electricity. While in Denmark, for example, consumers pay the highest annual average cost for electricity, this represents less than 1% of people's income. This comparison is illustrated in Table 3.1 and Figure 3.2.

Table 3.1. **Energy affordability for electricity, 2016**

Country	Average electricity tariff for households EUR/kWh	Average household income, EUR annually	Annual costs of electricity EUR annually	Share of the costs in household income %
Moldova**	0.092	3 474.30	117.92	3.39
Romania*	0.123	6 157.90	157.53	2.56
Turkey*	0.121	6 379.20	153.95	2.41
Ukraine	0.050	2 973.81	64.39	2.17
Albania*	0.084	4 972.79	106.68	2.15

Table 3.1. **Energy affordability for electricity, 2016** *(continued)*

Country	Average electricity tariff for households EUR/kWh	Average household income, EUR annually	Annual costs of electricity EUR annually	Share of the costs in household income %
Georgia	0.074	4 406.85	94.51	2.14
FYR of Macedonia*	0.083	5 880.34	105.79	1.80
Armenia	0.074	5 654.93	94.54	1.67
Bulgaria*	0.094	7 330.40	119.84	1.63
Latvia*	0.162	13 432.00	207.48	1.54
Montenegro*	0.097	8 570.40	123.93	1.45
Portugal*	0.230	21 931.00	293.60	1.34
Lithuania*	0.117	11 396.00	149.61	1.31
Hungary*	0.113	11 006.47	143.73	1.31
Serbia*	0.065	7 377.60	83.56	1.13
Greece*	0.172	19 570.20	220.13	1.12
Poland*	0.135	15 568.00	172.73	1.11
Croatia*	0.133	15 595.58	170.05	1.09
Kosovo*	0.059	7 120.00	75.63	1.06
Czech Republic*	0.142	17 221.36	181.55	1.05
Bosnia and Herzegovina*	0.084	10 433.43	107.83	1.03
Slovakia*	0.154	19 404.00	196.37	1.01
Germany*	0.298	41 288.00	380.35	0.92
Estonia*	0.124	17 340.40	158.17	0.91
Spain*	0.228	34 314.64	291.81	0.85
Italy*	0.234	38 664.24	298.96	0.77
Slovenia*	0.163	28 363.60	208.12	0.73
Belgium*	0.275	50 754.60	350.71	0.69
Russia	0.074	14 302.26	94.01	0.66
Denmark*	0.308	61 266.24	394.01	0.64
Cyprus*a	0.162	37 241.10	207.10	0.56
Ireland*	0.234	59 210.97	298.70	0.50
Austria*	0.201	53 730.60	256.80	0.48
Sweden*	0.196	53 544.39	250.67	0.47
United Kingdom*	0.183	50 063.33	233.93	0.47
France*	0.171	47 113.00	218.60	0.46
Malta*	0.127	36 431.10	162.77	0.45
Netherlands*	0.159	47 485.62	203.40	0.43
Finland*	0.155	49 902.30	197.39	0.40
Kyrgyzstan	0.010	3 413.25	12.38	0.36
Iceland*	0.148	61 601.80	188.83	0.31
Luxembourg*	0.170	81 121.00	216.94	0.27
Norway*	0.163	87 729.96	208.38	0.24
Liechtenstein*	0.168	91 361.60	214.38	0.23

Notes: a. Note by Turkey: The information in this document with reference to "Cyprus" relates to the southern part of the Island. There is no single authority representing both Turkish and Greek Cypriot people on the Island. Turkey recognises the Turkish Republic of Northern Cyprus (TRNC). Until a lasting and equitable solution is found within the context of the United Nations, Turkey shall preserve its position concerning the "Cyprus issue".

Note by all the European Union Member States of the OECD and the European Union: The Republic of Cyprus is recognised by all members of the United Nations with the exception of Turkey. The information in this document relates to the area under the effective control of the Government of the Republic of Cyprus.

Sources: *Eurostat http://ec.europa.eu/eurostat/statistics-explained/index.php/Electricity_price_statistics and **Eurostat: http://appsso.eurostat.ec.europa.eu/nui/show.do?dataset=ilc_di04&lang=en and www.statistica.md.
Georgia: www.telasi.ge/en/customers/tariffs. Kyrgyzstan: http://cbd.minjust.gov.kg/act/view/ru-ru/97149. Russia: www.mosenergosbyt.ru/website/content/conn/UCM/uuid/dDocName%3aMP047298. Ukraine: http://kyivenergo.ua/ru/tarifi. Data for all countries accessed on 8 April 2017.

Figure 3.2. **Energy affordability for electricity: Share of spending on electricity in disposable household income and average annual spending on electricity, in EUR**

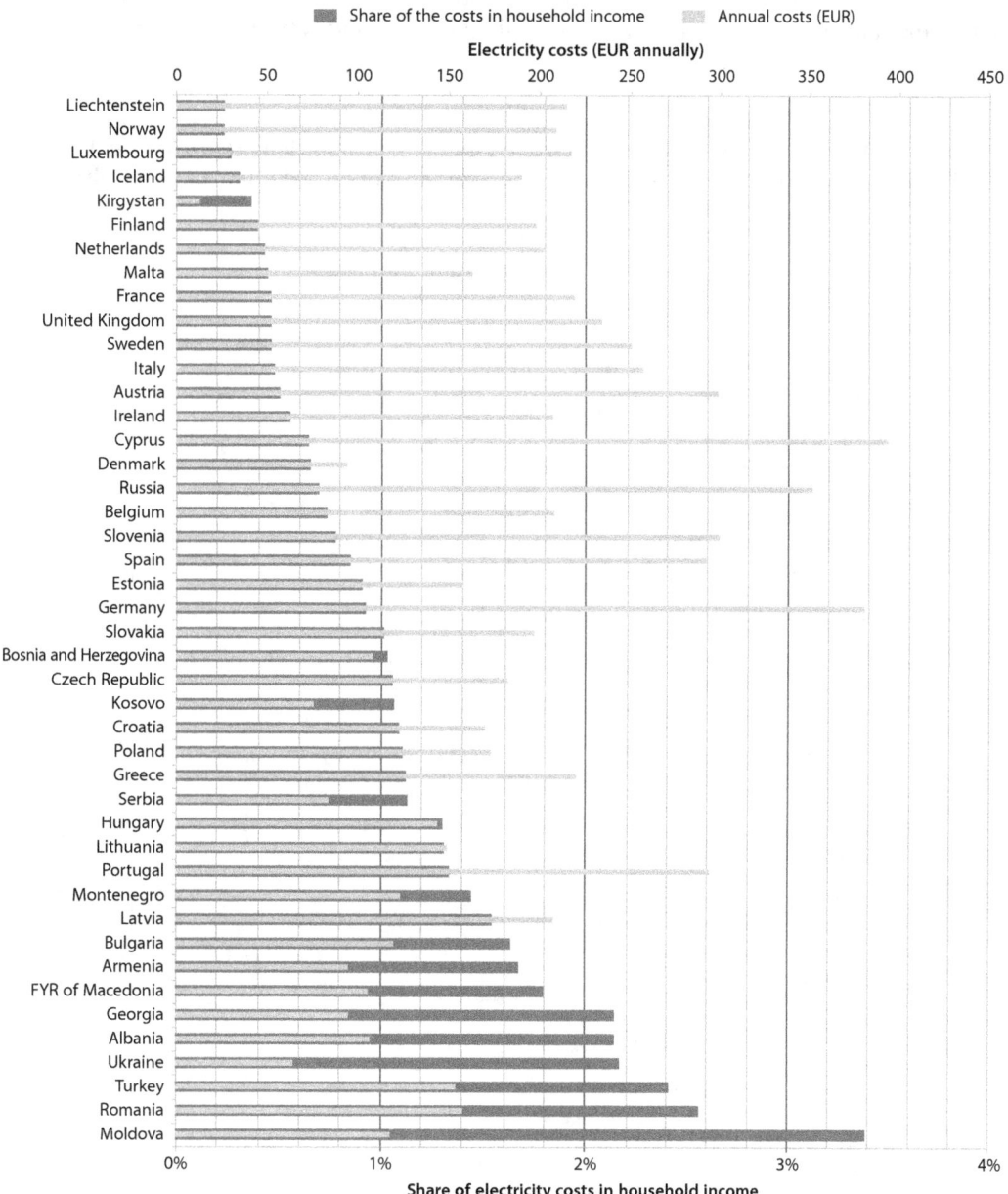

Sources: *Eurostat: http://ec.europa.eu/eurostat/statistics-explained/index.php/Electricity_price_statistics and **Eurostat: http://appsso.eurostat.ec.europa.eu/nui/show.do?dataset=ilc_di04&lang=en and www.statistica.md. Georgia: www.telasi.ge/en/customers/tariffs. Kyrgyzstan: http://cbd.minjust.gov.kg/act/view/ru-ru/97149. Russia: www.mosenergosbyt.ru/website/content/conn/UCM/uuid/dDocName%3aMP047298. Ukraine: http://kyivenergo.ua/ru/tarifi. Data for all countries accessed on 8 April 2017.

As the current consumption of electricity may be somewhat misleading, Figure 3.3 presents the same data but at a higher consumption level, which is more relevant to Moldovan cities, especially Chisinau. For this comparison, the average annual Italian consumption of 2 432 kWh per household was used. Italy, as an OECD country, is a good benchmark, as it has a moderate level of electricity consumption while, for example, the countries of Central and Eastern Europe have a much lower consumption than Moldova and are less relevant for this analysis. At this higher level of consumption, the share of the costs of electricity in household income in Moldova remains basically the same, and is the highest of the countries analysed.

Figure 3.3. **Energy affordability for electricity, higher consumption: Share of spending on electricity in disposable household income and average annual spending on electricity, EUR**

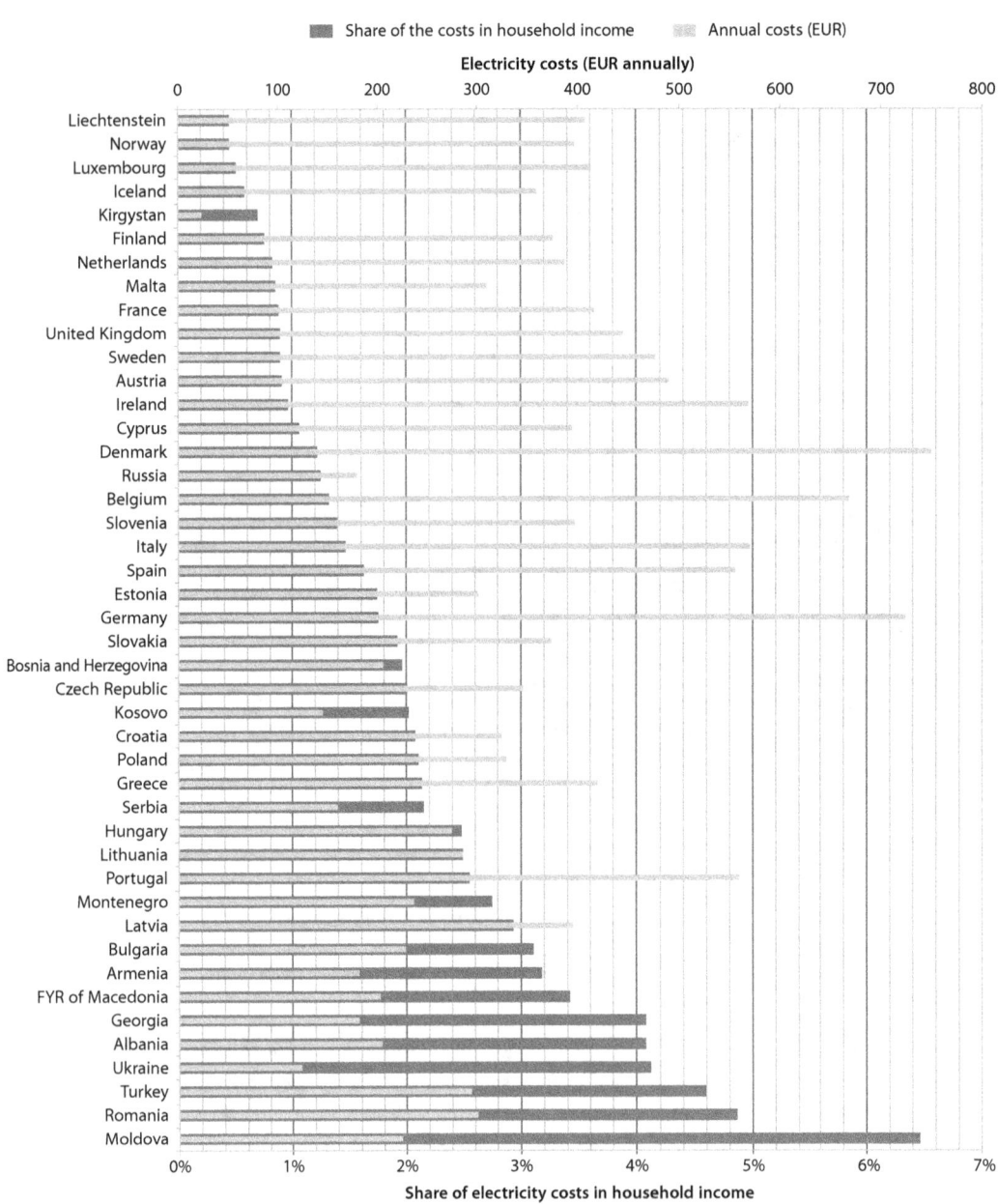

Sources: *Eurostat: http://ec.europa.eu/eurostat/statistics-explained/index.php/Electricity_price_statistics and **Eurostat: http://appsso.eurostat.ec.europa.eu/nui/show.do?dataset=ilc_di04&lang=en and www.statistica.md. Georgia: www.telasi.ge/en/customers/tariffs. Kyrgyzstan: http://cbd.minjust.gov.kg/act/view/ru-ru/97149. Russia: www.mosenergosbyt.ru/website/content/conn/UCM/uuid/dDocName%3aMP047298. Ukraine: http://kyivenergo.ua/ru/tarifi. Data for all countries accessed on 8 April 2017.

3.3. Natural gas for cooking

The analysis covers 33 countries, most of which are EU members, with a selected number of countries of South-Eastern Europe. Of the EaP countries detailed data were available only for Armenia, Georgia, Moldova and Ukraine. The natural gas prices vary from EUR 0.07 per kWh in the Russian Federation to EUR 0.1142 in Sweden.

Moldova is among the countries with the lowest natural gas prices for households (it is worth noting, however, the recent significant increase in gas tariffs in Ukraine in 2016). Moldova's prices are similar to those in Turkey and Bulgaria. Most of the EaP countries have set natural gas prices for household consumers at a level higher than Moldova's. Natural gas prices for household consumers higher than those in Moldova can be observed in the EU countries and in the Russian Federation.

Energy affordability of natural gas consumption, like electricity affordability, typically compares the average annual cost of natural gas consumption for the average household with average annual household income. It is difficult to distinguish the consumption of the natural gas for cooking only and for cooking and other purposes. It was assumed that average consumption for cooking totals only 15 m^3 per month, or 2 027.34 kWh per year.[3] It should be noted that this level of consumption reflects the consumption of gas used for cooking purposes only. For the sake of comparison and facility, the same consumption level is used here for all countries in the dataset.

Analysis of higher gas consumption, where gas is used for both cooking and heating, is also possible. However, as most countries have introduced a volumetric price (and only a small number of countries still maintain a small fixed tariff), this will bring the analysis to the same conclusions.

Taking into account the average annual income, the least expensive countries are Luxembourg and the Russian Federation, where natural gas bills account for only 0.1% of disposable household income. In most countries, natural gas consumption accounts for less than 1% of household disposable income. The two countries where the population pays the highest price as a share of its disposable income are Moldova, at 1.72%, and Ukraine at 1.62% (before the gas tariff increase of 2016). The comparison is illustrated in Table 3.2 and Figure 3.4.

Table 3.2. **Energy affordability for natural gas, 2016**

Country	Average natural gas price for households, EUR/kWh	Average household income, EUR annually	Annual costs of natural gas, EUR annually	Share of the costs in household income %
Moldova**	0.030	3 474.30	59.81	1.72
Ukraine	0.024	2 973.81	48.25	1.62
Romania*	0.032	6 157.90	65.48	1.06
Turkey*	0.030	6 379.20	61.02	0.96
Serbia*	0.033	7 377.60	66.09	0.90
Bulgaria*	0.031	7 330.40	63.05	0.86
Georgia	0.017	4 406.85	34.88	0.79
Portugal*	0.082	21 931.00	165.23	0.75
Lithuania*	0.039	11 396.00	78.46	0.69
Greece*	0.065	19 570.20	132.18	0.68

Table 3.2. **Energy affordability for natural gas, 2016** *(continued)*

Country	Average natural gas price for households, EUR/kWh	Average household income, EUR annually	Annual costs of natural gas, EUR annually	Share of the costs in household income %
Hungary*	0.036	11 006.47	72.98	0.66
Czech Republic*	0.056	17 221.36	114.14	0.66
Bosnia and Herzegovina*	0.034	10 392.57	68.12	0.66
Latvia*	0.041	13 432.00	82.31	0.61
Armenia	0.017	5 654.93	34.46	0.61
Poland*	0.044	15 568.00	89.41	0.57
Spain*	0.086	34 314.64	173.74	0.51
Croatia*	0.037	15 595.58	75.01	0.48
Slovakia*	0.045	19 404.00	90.22	0.46
Italy*	0.084	38 664.24	169.89	0.44
Sweden*	0.114	53 544.39	231.52	0.43
Slovenia*	0.056	28 363.60	114.14	0.40
Estonia*	0.033	17 340.40	66.50	0.38
Netherlands*	0.081	47 485.62	163.81	0.34
Germany*	0.064	41 288.00	130.16	0.32
France*	0.068	47 113.00	137.05	0.29
Austria*	0.067	53 730.60	136.64	0.25
Denmark*	0.074	61 266.24	150.23	0.25
Ireland*	0.068	59 210.97	137.45	0.23
Belgium*	0.053	50 754.60	108.26	0.21
United Kingdom*	0.050	50 063.33	101.57	0.20
Liechtenstein*	0.082	91 361.60	166.85	0.18
Russia	0.008	14 302.26	16.19	0.11
Luxembourg*	0.042	81 121.00	84.74	0.10

Sources: *Eurostat: http://ec.europa.eu/eurostat/statistics-explained/index.php/Natural_gas_price_statistics
**Eurostat: http://appsso.eurostat.ec.europa.eu/nui/show.do?dataset=ilc_di04&lang=en and www.statistica.md.
Georgia: www.newsgeorgia.ge/tarify-na-prirodnyj-gaz-v-gruzii-mogut-uvelichitsya/.
Kyrgyzstan: stat.kg/en/statistics/ceny-i-tarify/.
Russia: http://energovopros.ru/spravochnik/gazosnabzhenie/tarify-na-gaz/moskva/41171/.
Ukraine: http://index.minfin.com.ua/tarif/gas/.
Data for all countries accessed on 10 April 2017.

Figure 3.4. **Energy affordability for natural gas: Share of spending on natural gas in disposable household income and average annual spending for natural gas, in EUR**

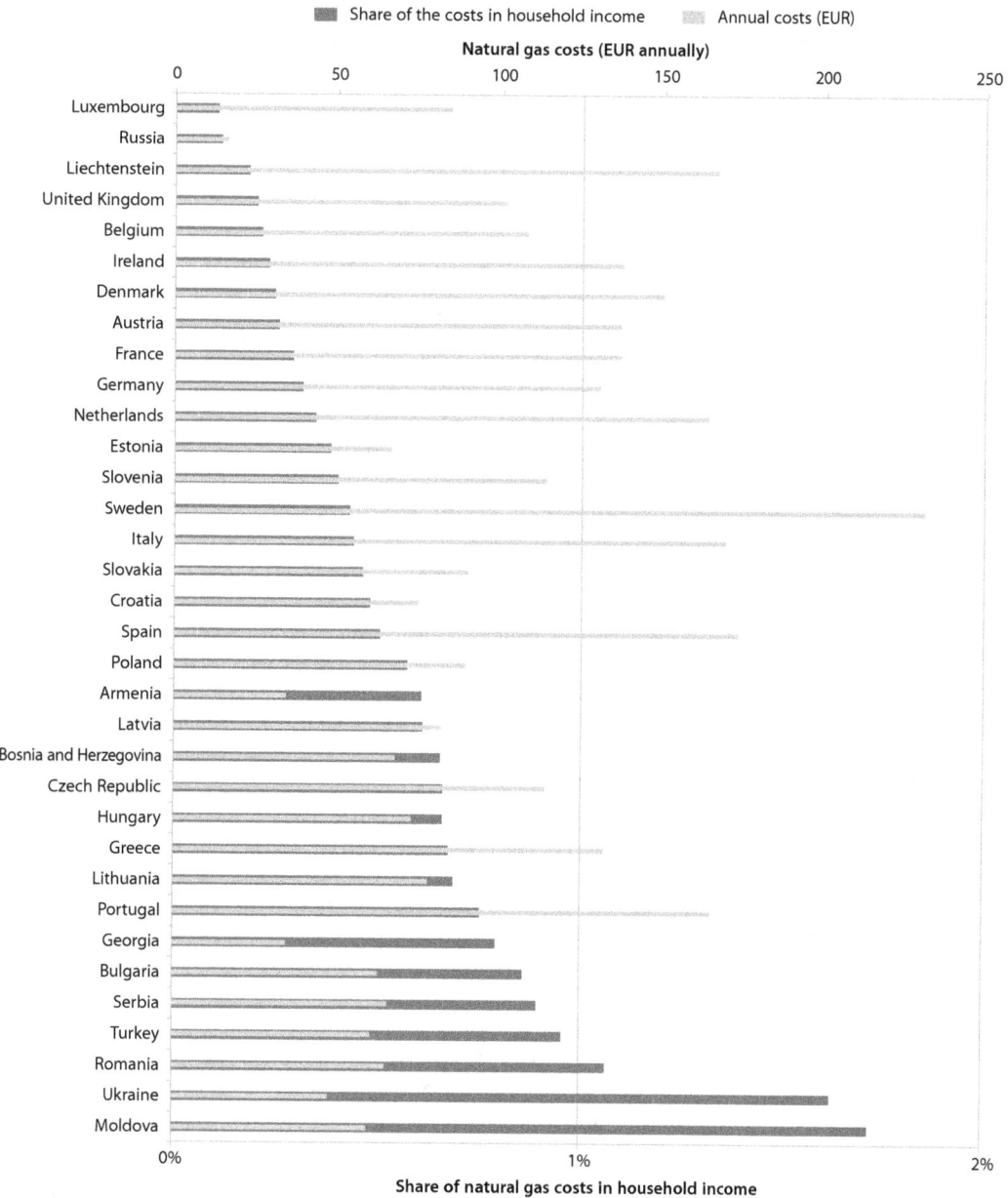

Sources: *Eurostat: http://ec.europa.eu/eurostat/statistics-explained/index.php/Natural_gas_price_statistics
**Eurostat: http://appsso.eurostat.ec.europa.eu/nui/show.do?dataset=ilc_di04&lang=en and www.statistica.md.
Georgia: www.newsgeorgia.ge/tarify-na-prirodnyj-gaz-v-gruzii-mogut-uvelichitsya/.
Kyrgyzstan: stat.kg/en/statistics/ceny-i-tarify/.
Russia: http://energovopros.ru/spravochnik/gazosnabzhenie/tarify-na-gaz/moskva/41171/.
Ukraine: http://index.minfin.com.ua/tarif/gas/.
Data for all countries accessed on 10 April 2017.

Figure 3.5. **Energy affordability for natural gas for cooking and heating: Share of spending on gas in disposable household income and average annual spending for natural gas, in EUR**

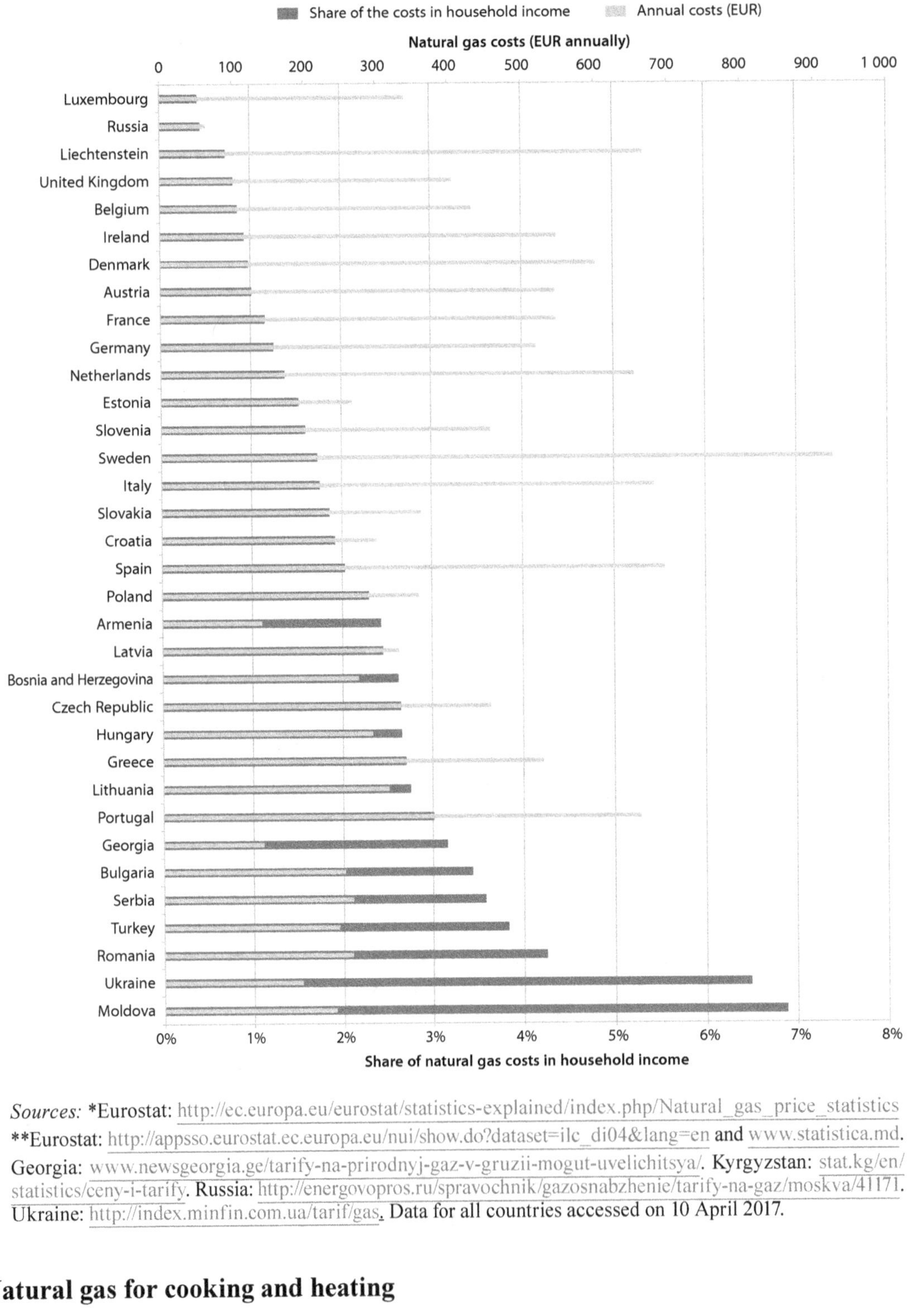

[Bar chart showing Share of the costs in household income and Annual costs (EUR) for countries including Luxembourg, Russia, Liechtenstein, United Kingdom, Belgium, Ireland, Denmark, Austria, France, Germany, Netherlands, Estonia, Slovenia, Sweden, Italy, Slovakia, Croatia, Spain, Poland, Armenia, Latvia, Bosnia and Herzegovina, Czech Republic, Hungary, Greece, Lithuania, Portugal, Georgia, Bulgaria, Serbia, Turkey, Romania, Ukraine, Moldova. Top axis: Natural gas costs (EUR annually) 0–1000. Bottom axis: Share of natural gas costs in household income 0%–8%.]

Sources: *Eurostat: http://ec.europa.eu/eurostat/statistics-explained/index.php/Natural_gas_price_statistics
**Eurostat: http://appsso.eurostat.ec.europa.eu/nui/show.do?dataset=ilc_di04&lang=en and www.statistica.md. Georgia: www.newsgeorgia.ge/tarify-na-prirodnyj-gaz-v-gruzii-mogut-uvelichitsya/. Kyrgyzstan: stat.kg/en/statistics/ceny-i-tarify. Russia: http://energovopros.ru/spravochnik/gazosnabzhenie/tarify-na-gaz/moskva/41171. Ukraine: http://index.minfin.com.ua/tarif/gas. Data for all countries accessed on 10 April 2017.

3.4. Natural gas for cooking and heating

As the consumption of natural gas for cooking only is rather low, Figure 3.5 shows the recalculations for higher gas consumption, including the use of gas for both cooking and heating. The average annual consumption of 8 109.36 kWh[4] per household was used in this comparison. Natural gas consumption for heating varies across countries and depends on three variables:

- how affordable natural gas is
- climate conditions that determine the level of natural gas consumption
- energy consumption at the level of an apartment or a house that depends on building insulation and other energy efficiency measures, especially if energy can be controlled.

For comparison, the same consumption level is used for all countries in this analysis.

3.5. Heating

In general, the district heating sector is narrower than the electricity and natural gas market. In most countries, district heating is available in selected cities only and tariffs are often regulated at the local level. For this reason, only a few countries were selected for this part of the analysis.

Prices for heat energy vary across countries, from the lowest, in the Kyrgyz Republic (EUR 0.01 per kWh) to the highest, in Austria (EUR 0.09 per kWh). At EUR 0.049 per kWh, Moldova's average heat energy price is not particularly low and falls in the middle of the price range. It is higher than the price in all other EaP and CA countries but lower than in countries such as Estonia, Germany or Austria.

The same energy affordability analysis is done here as for electricity and gas for cooking and heating, and the same annual consumption of 8 000 kWh was used for comparison. The analysis shows that among all countries analysed, Moldova's population spends the highest share of its household disposable income on heat energy. The comparison is illustrated by data provided in Table 3.3 and Figure 3.6.

Table 3.3. **Energy affordability for heating, 2016**

Country	Average price for heating, EUR/kWh	Average household income, EUR annually	Annual costs of heat energy, EUR annually	Share of the costs in household income, %
Moldova	0.049390548	3 474.30	395.1244	11.37
Ukraine	0.040937107	2 973.81	327.4969	11.01
Serbia	630.3924 [a]	7 377.60	630.3924	8.54
Czech Republic	0.101444043	17 221.36	811.5523	4.71
Romania	0.030839725	6 157.90	246.7178	4.01
Kyrgyzstan	0.012196475	3 413.25	97.5718	2.86
Estonia	0.0597	17 340.40	477.6	2.75
Poland	0.032414816	15 568.00	416.3185	2.67
Armenia	0.018669964	5 654.93	149.3597	2.64
Russia	0.027813805	14 302.26	222.5104	1.56
Germany	0.08	41 288.00	640	1.55
Austria	0.08724	53 730.60	697.92	1.30

Note: a. In Serbia, heating tariff are calculated per m², and are not volumetric, due to the lack of metering even at the entrance of buildings. Thus, the tariff represents an annual cost for a 55 m² apartment.

Sources: Authors' research based on data provided by the National Agency for Energy Regulation of Moldova and http://statistica.md. Ukraine: kyivenergo.ua/ru/te-home/opalennya. Serbia: www.beoelektrane.rs/wp-content/uploads/2011/01/A-Sl-List-BGD-br-56-od-30-septembar-2015-Saglasnost-gradonacelnika-na-cene-toplotne-energije.jpg. Czech Republic: www.ptas.cz/cs/dodavky-tepla/ceny-a-obchodni-podminky/ceniky/. Romania: www.radet.ro/tarife-radet-bucuresti.php. Kyrgyzstan: cbd.minjust.gov.kg/act/view/ru-ru/97149. Estonia: www.utilitas.ee/soojuse_hinnad/. Poland: www.energiadlawarszawy.pl/sites/default/files/pismo_warszawa_zmiana_taryfy_2_0.pdf. Armenia: www.habitat.org/sites/default/files/heating20-armenia_uh_analysis.pdf. Russia: depr.mos.ru/upload_local/iblock/e2b/e2bc9ae862273b6bfa7fdff55aa46b50/848_pp.pdf. Germany: https://wärme.vattenfall.de/berlin/produkte/fernwaerme-natur-mix. Austria: www.energie-graz.at/upload/file/Preisblatt%20Fernwaerme_2016_screen.pdf. Data for all countries accessed on 12 April 2017.

Figure 3.6. **Energy affordability for heating: Share of spending on heating in disposable household income and average annual spending for heating, in EUR**

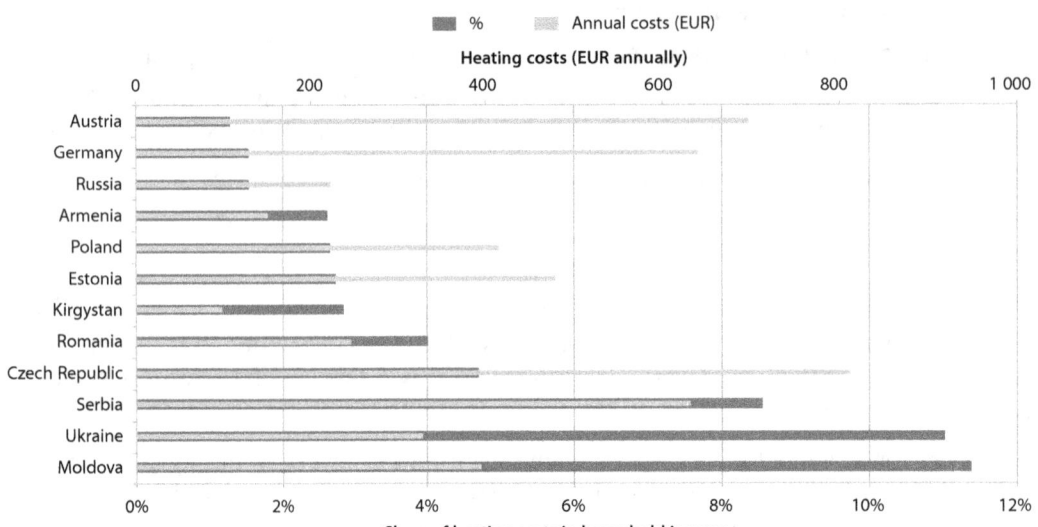

Sources: *Authors' research based on data from National Agency for Energy Regulation of Moldova and http://statistica.md.
Ukraine: kyivenergo.ua/ru/te-home/opalennya. Serbia: www.beoelektrane.rs/wp-content/uploads/2011/01/A-Sl-List-BGD-br-56-od-30-septembar-2015-Saglasnost-gradonacelnika-na-cene-toplotne-energije.jpg. Czech Republic: www.ptas.cz/cs/dodavky-tepla/ceny-a-obchodni-podminky/ceniky/. Romania: www.radet.ro/tarife-radet-bucuresti.php. Kyrgyzstan: cbd.minjust.gov.kg/act/view/ru-ru/97149. Estonia: www.utilitas.ee/soojuse_hinnad/. Poland: www.energiadlawarszawy.pl/sites/default/files/pismo_warszawa_zmiana_taryfy_2_0.pdf. Armenia: www.habitat.org/sites/default/files/heating20-armenia_uh_analysis.pdf. Russia: depr.mos.ru/upload_local/iblock/e2b/e2bc9ae862273b6bfa7fdff55aa46b50/848_pp.pdf. Germany: https://wärme.vattenfall.de/berlin/produkte/fernwaerme-natur-mix. Austria: www.energie-graz.at/upload/file/Preisblatt%20Fernwaerme_2016_screen.pdf. Data for all countries accessed on 12 April 2017.

3.6. Combined use of electricity and natural gas for cooking and heating

The analysis below summarises the costs of electricity and natural gas that are used for cooking and for heating purposes and discusses the use of combined energy sources that are typically used by households. This analysis is presented in Figure 3.7.

In terms of annual costs of electricity and gas, Moldovan households are not among the top spenders, but as a percentage of household disposable income, the costs are by far the highest of all the other countries in the sample.

3.7. Conclusions

The share of household income spent on electricity and heating is the best measure of how tariff increases for energy services might affect poorer households. The foregoing comparative analysis shows that in terms of household spending on energy carriers – electricity and natural gas for cooking and heating – Moldova is among the most expensive countries in Europe, as well as in the EaP and CA regions. Energy and electricity sector reforms will need to account for the fact that affordability thresholds could be exceeded and that customers would need to take measures to reduce their energy expenditure. Vulnerable households will need to be protected to ensure that they should not bear the significant costs of sector reforms.

Figure 3.7. **Energy affordability for the combined use of electricity and natural gas for cooking and heating: Share of spending on electricity and natural gas for cooking and heating in disposable household income, in EUR**

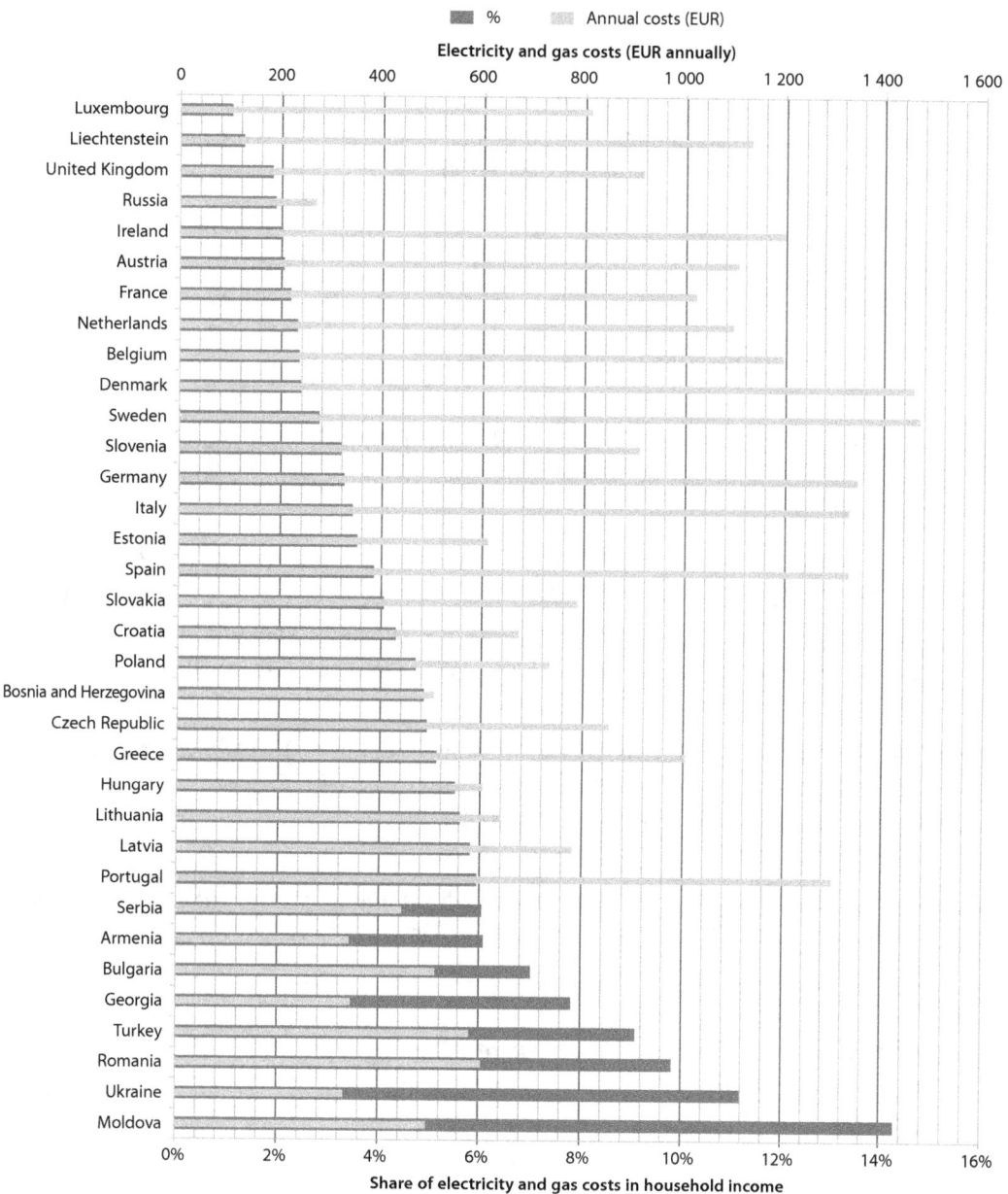

Source: Authors' own calculations based on Eurostat (2017a, 2017b).

Notes

1. EC (2017).
2. Eurostat. http://cbd.minjust.gov.kg/act/view/ru-ru/97149.
3. Calorific value of 11.263 kWh per cubic metre.
4. Equivalent of natural gas consumption of 60 m³ per month or 147 kWh per m² per year for a 55 m² apartment (without consumption of electricity).

References

Black Sea Press News Agency (2017), "Natural gas tariffs in Georgia can raise", 22 February 2017, Tbilisi, www.newsgeorgia.ge/tarify-na-prirodnyj-gaz-v-gruzii-mogut-uvelichitsya/.

Cabinet of Ministers of Ukraine (2015), *Decree No. 220 of 26 February 2015 on Electricity Tariffs for the Population*, KiyvEnergo, Kyiv, http://kyivenergo.ua/ru/tarifi.

Cabinet of Ministers of Ukraine (2017), *Decree No. 187 of 22 May 2017 on Retail Tariffs of Natural Gas for the Population*, Ministry of Finance of Ukraine, Kyiv, http://index.minfin.com.ua/tarif/gas/.

Committee on Prices and Tariffs of the Moscow Region (2016), *Order No. 203-p of 16 December 2016 on Setting Electricity Prices (Tariffs) for the Population of the Moscow Region for 2017*, City of Krasnogorsk, www.mosenergosbyt.ru/website/content/conn/UCM/uuid/dDocName%3aMP047298.

EC (2017), *VAT Rates Applied in the Member States of the European Union – Situation as of 1st January 2017*, European Commission, Brussels, https://ec.europa.eu/taxation_customs/sites/taxation/files/resources/documents/taxation/vat/how_vat_works/rates/vat_rates_en.pdf.

EnergoVOPROS. Ru (2018), *Tariffs on Gas in Moscow. In Force as of 1 January 2018*, EnergoVOPROS.ru, http://energovopros.ru/spravochnik/gazosnabzhenie/tarify-na-gaz/moskva/41171/.

Energy Group Utilitas (2017), *District Heating, Energy Group Utilitas of Estonia*, Tallinn, utilitas.ee/soojuse_hinnad/.

Eurostat (2018), *Mean and Medium Income by Household Type – EU-SILC Survey*, updated on 15 February 2018, Eurostat, Luxembourg. http://appsso.eurostat.ec.europa.eu/nui/show.do?dataset=ilc_di04&lang=en.

Eurostat (2017a), *Statistics Explained, Electricity Price Statistics, Updated November 2017*, Eurostat, Luxembourg, http://ec.europa.eu/eurostat/statistics-explained/index.php/Electricity_price_statistics.

Eurostat (2017b), *Statistics Explained, Natural Gas Price Statistics, Updated November 2017*, Eurostat, Luxembourg, http://ec.europa.eu/eurostat/statistics-explained/index.php/Natural_gas_price_statistics.

Ghukasyan, A. and A. Pasoyan (2006), *Armenian Urban Heating Policy Assessment*, USAID, Yerevan, www.habitat.org/sites/default/files/heating20-armenia_uh_analysis.pdf.

GoM (2013), *Decree No. 102 on Energy Strategy of the Republic of Moldova until 2030*, Government of Moldova, Chisinau.

Mayor of Belgrade (2015*)*, *Decision on the Change of Prices for Heat Energy Supply by the Communal Enterprise "Belgrade Energy"*, September 2015, Belgrade City Administration, www.beoelektrane.rs/wp-content/uploads/2011/01/A-Sl-List-BGD-br-56-od-30-septembar-2015-Saglasnost-gradonacelnika-na-cene-toplotne-energije.jpg.

Ministry of Justice of the Kyrgyz Republic (2014), *Decree No. 660 of 20 November 2014 on Approving the Mid-Term Tariff Policy of the Kyrgyz Republic for Electricity and Heat Energy for 2014-2017*, Centralised Database of Legal Information of the Kyrgyz Republic, Government of Kyrgyz Republic, Bishkek, http://cbd.minjust.gov.kg/act/view/ru-ru/97149.

NCSRESCS (2017), *Decree No. 1 536 of 28 December 2017 on Tariffs for Centralised Heating in Force of 31 December 2017*, National Commission for State Regulation of Energy Supply and Communal Services, Kyiv, kyivenergo.ua/ru/te-home/opalennya.

NSC of KR, *Prices and Tariffs Database*, National Statistical Committee of the Kyrgyz Republic, Bishkek. stat.kg/en/statistics/ceny-i-tarify/.

Prazska teplarenska, *Heat Supply for the City of Prague*, Prazska teplarenska (Thermal Energy Supplier in Prague), www.ptas.cz/cs/dodavky-tepla/ceny-a-obchodni-podminky/ceniky/.

RADET (2017), *Thermal Energy Billing Tariff According to HCGMB No. 472 of 28 September 2017*, Autonomous Distribution of Heat Energy, Bucharest, www.radet.ro/tarife-radet-bucuresti.php.

Telasi, *Tariffs for Electricity, Tbilisi, Georgia*. www.telasi.ge/en/customers/tariffs.

Vattenfall (2017), *Green Prospects for Heat Customers*, Vattenfall, Berlin, https://wärme.vattenfall.de/berlin/produkte/fernwaerme-natur-mix.

VEOLIA (2017), *Current Heat Prices and Rates in Use by Veolia Energia Warsaw S.A. as of 17 March 2017*, VEOLIA, Warsaw. www.energiadlawarszawy.pl/sites/default/files/pismo_warszawa_zmiana_taryfy_2_0.pdf.

World Energy Council, *Energy Efficiency Indicators Database*, https://www.worldenergy.org/data/efficiency-indicators/.

Chapter 4

Avoiding energy poverty in Moldova

Based on the review of measures aimed at protecting customers at risk of energy poverty that are used in the European Union and elsewhere, this chapter identifies possible measures that can be implemented in Moldova. The advantages and disadvantages of these measures are then analysed in detail. As a result, six compensation measures are selected for further modelling and analysis.

4.1. Overview of possible protection measures

Before looking at specific protection measures, it is important to introduce distinctions in the definitions of energy poverty and energy affordability. While there is no universally accepted definition of energy affordability, the concept is based on the comparison between energy spending and income. Low energy affordability implies high spending and low income. One definition of energy affordability is a household's ability to pay for necessary levels of energy consumption within normal spending patterns. Energy poverty, on the other hand, refers to situations where households lack access to modern energy services (especially in lower-income countries) and to low energy affordability combined with low energy efficiency (Pye et al., 2015).

The most important caveat in discussing potential measures is that effective policy to protect customers at risk of energy poverty should be based on both preventive and curative elements. This implies that there should not be just one measure, but that the policy should include a suite of measures designed to bring relief while alleviating the causes of energy poverty. Any policy aimed at relieving energy poverty should include a mix of financial, investment support and consumer support measures.

Financial measures: *Support payments to the most vulnerable segments of the population.*

A national programme could be set up to provide support payments (general welfare payments) for population segments at risk of energy poverty. Because the administrative costs of such a programme can be very high, using an existing measure of poverty rather than creating a new one is recommended. At the same time, a blanket measure that covers all people consuming, for example, less than 50% of the national average in heat energy should not be used in Moldova, due to the problems with cash flows of district heating companies. A rapid decrease in heat consumption would only create more financial challenges for the heat industry.

This measure could be developed for the medium term to support customers who could either use the support for a partial bill payment, or towards energy-efficiency investments, such as thermal renovation of dwellings or replacement of inefficient home appliances. This is the approach generally used in many countries, both in the European Union (EU) as well as in Moldova's more immediate neighbours. For example, in Ukraine, a transition for energy-efficiency reforms is planned, towards "subsidy monetisation" where the customer will choose how to spend the energy subsidy, either on energy-efficiency investments, or to cover the cost of energy services, or both. This possibility was also discussed in the review on international practices.

Investment support: *Energy efficiency*

As a preventive measure, an energy-efficiency programme could be developed for customers at risk. This could include a programme with a mix of grants and loans for vulnerable customers, to help them make thermal retrofits of dwellings or replace outdated and inefficient home appliances. At the same time, a non-targeted programme of energy efficiency retrofits and appliance replacement could be implemented for multi-family dwellings.

Consumer support measures: *Disconnection safeguards*

Those customers identified as at risk for energy poverty could be protected from automatic disconnection from service. As disconnection is rarely used in Moldova, formalising this policy for at-risk customers should not be controversial to implement.

Information measures: *Information and awareness campaigns*

The national energy regulator of Moldova, the Agency for Energy Regulation (ANRE) could launch an information campaign regarding transparent billing of heating and electricity services and energy-efficiency certification of buildings and appliances. At the regional or district (*rayon*) level, information points could be established to disseminate information about energy efficiency.

4.2. Identification of protection measures to be modelled and tested

To test the potential effectiveness of the proposed protection measures, these measures need to be defined in sufficient detail, which will also enable their modelling. The proposed customer support and information measures are not modelled in this study, as their impact is difficult to measure and to reflect in a dynamic model. Regardless of the selected financial and investment support measures, supplementary consumer support and information measures should be made.

In all reviewed support systems, where income testing is used, vulnerable households are identified, using the following indicators (each independently):[1]

- *10% rule* – a household is considered in energy poverty when it spends more than 10% of its disposable income (including other benefits) on energy services (gas, fuel, electricity, heating) – example: Republic of Ireland

- *15% rule* – as above, but a threshold of 15% modified rule as in the Republic of Ireland

- *10% fuel rule* – a household is considered in energy poverty when it spends more than 10% of its disposable income (including other benefits) on fuel – example: England

- *15% fuel rule* – as above, but a threshold of 15% modified rule as in England

- *5/10 rule* – a household is considered vulnerable (and in need of assistance) if it spends more than 5% of its disposable income (with benefits) on electricity and 10% on gas – example: Italy.

The income-testing method is easier to implement, but does not recognise people who are wealthy who may have a lot of capital (for example, they own expensive property) but at the same time, have a low annual income. For this reason, instead of using income testing, some countries prefer to use the means-testing approach. Means-testing checks not only people's income but their assets. One way to check this information is to ask people to prepare self-declarations and randomly verify the declarations.

Based on the above examples, the government of Moldova needs to identify the optimal indicator for defining energy poverty and thus the group of people who will eventually benefit from government support. The main criterion in selecting the best indicator should be the indicator that shows the lowest cost per vulnerable household served.

> ### Box 4.1. **Overview of support programme in Chisinau**
>
> The energy support programme in Chisinau described in this box serves as an example of social policies used in Moldova. Currently, families can qualify for support if their average monthly income does not exceed MDL 3 000 per person. The compensation for payments for energy resources is as follows:
>
> - For centralised heating, 40% of the amount calculated according to the heating tariff in force;
> - For domestic hot water, 40% of the calculated tariff for thermal energy;
> - For natural gas, electricity, wood and coal used for heating, MDL 450 per month per family;
> - For natural gas, electricity, wood and coal used by soldiers, MDL 900 per month.
>
> Table 4.1 provides programme data for the past several years (2008-13).
>
> Table 4.1. **Energy support programme, Chisinau, 2008-13**
>
> | Season | Number of families benefitting | Sum of benefits, MDL thousand | Average per family MDL |
> |---|---|---|---|
> | 2008-2009 | 19 398 | 22 851 | 1 178.01 |
> | 2009-2010 | 30 136 | 40 933 | 1 358.29 |
> | 2010-2011 | 37 085 | 67 518 | 1 820.63 |
> | 2011-2012 | 38 199 | 77 093 | 2 018.20 |
> | 2012-2013 (March) | 33 339 | 68 666 | 2 026.20 |
>
> In addition, and in order to qualify, potential beneficiaries need to supply a proof of family composition, housing and heating certificates, bills for payment of communal services, extracts from personal accounts, certificate of annual salary from the place of work, and other documents confirming the need for compensation.
>
> *Source:* Municipal Council of the City of Chisinau (2016).

As part of this study, a number of financial and investment measures were considered for further analysis and modelling. These measures include:

- *Uniform lump sum transfer to all households – without stipulating how funds are to be used.* With this measure, each family in Moldova receives a lump sum transfer, effectively as income support. The level of income support to all households should be calculated so as to reduce by 50% the number of households experiencing extreme poverty.[2] There is no link between the payments and the financial stress caused by energy and electricity bills. Alternatively, an indirect link can be made by making the lump sum payments seasonal – for example, during the winter months or, alternatively, during the months in which the district heating company provides heat (based on a consecutive number of cold days). This approach increases the likelihood that the support payments will be used to offset the impact of increased utility costs. Seasonal payments are less applicable to electricity costs, unless electricity is the main source of heating during winter months. This is not common in Moldova.

- *Uniform lump sum transfer to all households – stipulating that it must be used for energy-efficiency investments.* Under this measure, each family in Moldova receives a lump sum transfer, effectively as income support, on the condition that they use it to reduce the energy costs of the household (for example, through energy-efficiency investments, such as replacement of heating sources, thermal renovation, replacement of inefficient appliances or purchase of efficient appliances). The level of income support to all households should be calculated so as to reduce the number of households experiencing extreme poverty by 50%.[3] These payments should not be seasonal, as this would limit their use towards energy-efficiency investments.

- *Income-tested transfer to all households – without stipulating how funds are to be used.* With this measure, only vulnerable families in Moldova receive a lump sum transfer, effectively as income support. The level of income support to vulnerable households should be calculated to reduce by 50% the number of households experiencing extreme poverty.[4] There is no link between the payments and the financial stress caused by energy and electricity bills. Alternatively, an indirect link can be made by making the lump sum payments seasonal – for example, during the winter months or during the months in which the district heating company provides heat (based on a consecutive number of cold days). This increases the likelihood that the support payments will be used to offset the impact of utility costs. Seasonal payments are less applicable to electricity costs, unless electricity is the main source of heating during winter months. This is not a common practice in Moldova. This measure was actually tested in the model for households earning MDL 4 000 per month or less.

- *Income-tested transfer to all households – with stipulation for use on energy-efficiency investments.* With this measure, only vulnerable families in Moldova receive a lump sum transfer, effectively as income support, on the condition that they use it to reduce the energy costs of the household (for example, through energy-efficiency investments such as replacement of heating sources, thermal renovation, replacement of inefficient appliances, or purchase of efficient appliances). The level of income support to all households should be calculated to reduce by 50% the number of households experiencing extreme poverty.[5] These payments should not be seasonal, as this would limit their use for energy-efficiency investments.

- *Value-added tax (VAT) relief, energy costs above x% of household income* – households receive VAT relief if energy costs (electricity, gas, district heating) exceed x% of total disposable household income. Thus, vulnerable households get a VAT rebate if their energy expenditures exceed a certain percentage. In the model, various percentages are tested. This measure puts more money in the hands of low-income families but it does not ensure that the VAT relief will be spent on curative measures (such as increasing energy efficiency).

- *VAT relief, energy costs above x% of household income, voucher system* – this measure is similar to the previous one, but with vulnerable households receiving vouchers they can use to pay their energy costs. This measure is cheaper than the VAT relief measure, as it has lower administrative costs.

- *VAT relief, incremental protection* – with this measure, income-tested households receive compensation for any incremental VAT increase for utility services (electricity, gas, district heating, etc.). Thus, vulnerable households pay a fixed VAT rate and are compensated for any future increase in VAT for these services. This measure effectively puts more money in the hands of low-income families, but it does not ensure that the VAT relief will be spent on curative measures (such as increasing energy efficiency).

- *VAT relief, 0% rate* – with this measure, income-tested households pay a 0% VAT rate for utility services (electricity, gas, district heating, etc.). Such households would receive a voucher showing their qualified status. This measure effectively puts more money in the hands of low-income families but it does not ensure that the VAT relief will be spent on curative measures (such as increasing energy efficiency).

- *VAT relief, mixed rates* – with this measure, income-tested households pay a 0% VAT rate on energy consumption up to a pre-determined basic/minimal level. For additional consumption, they pay the normal VAT rate. This applies to utility services (electricity, gas, district heating, etc.). Such households receive a voucher showing their qualified status and a separate tariff group is established for them. This measure effectively puts more money in the hands of low-income families but it does not ensure that the VAT relief will be spent on curative measures (such as increasing energy efficiency). The measure, however, provides incentives to reduce consumption by making households consume less energy, which allows them to qualify for the 0% threshold. Importantly, this measure would be aimed at addressing energy poverty without benefiting wealthier households that do not need support.

- *VAT relief and cost compensation exceeding x% of household income* – under this measure, vulnerable households receive both VAT relief and compensation of expenditure for energy services exceeding $x\%$ of disposable household income.

- *Income test, VAT compensation* – VAT rebate for families earning less than MDL 4 000 per month.

- *Retrofit investment programmes, non-targeted* – under this measure, grants, loans and tax incentives are provided for investments in energy-efficiency measures (such as building renovation and thermal retrofits). The programme is not targeted at vulnerable consumers.

- *Retrofit investment programmes, targeted* – under this measure, grants, loans and tax incentives are provided for investments in energy-efficiency measures (such as building renovation and thermal retrofits). The programme is targeted to vulnerable consumers.

- *Appliance grant programmes, non-targeted* – under this measure, grants are provided for the replacement of energy-inefficient appliances. The programme is not targeted at vulnerable consumers.

- *Appliance grant programmes, targeted* – under this measure, grants are provided for the replacement of energy-inefficient appliances. The programme targets vulnerable consumers.

4.3. Main results of the modelling of the proposed protection measures

The advantages and disadvantages of the above measures and the conclusions from the modelling are summarised in Table 4.2.

Table 4.2. **Financial and investment measures**

Measure	Advantages	Disadvantages	Conclusion
No compensation	• No additional costs to government or service provider	• No relief to vulnerable households	**Baseline scenario for comparison**
Uniform lump sum transfer to all households without targeting energy-efficiency investments [a]	• Comparatively lower administrative costs per family to implement and administer • Could alleviate extreme poverty • May increase consumer purchases and overall consumption patterns	• Households that do not need support benefit from untargeted subsidy • Without designation for gas, heat and electricity payments, no incentive to implement energy-saving measures, such as thermal modernisation or replacement of heating sources (although increased consumption may result in replacement of inefficient appliances) • Despite lower administrative costs per family, this measure involves an additional layer of bureaucracy to oversee payments • Payment per family likely to be small, due to national budget constraints • Does not include a mix of policy instruments (identifying poor people, providing incentives for energy efficiency investments) and does not ensure that the source of vulnerability to energy poverty is addressed • Depending on the size of payments, may entail a disincentive to work	**Seasonal, lump sum payments are not modelled.** Currently, ineffective way (cost per person too high) and very costly for the budget to provide relief to at-risk families. Energy and electricity sectors in Moldova currently do not meet preconditions for this kind of monetisation (see description of measures in other countries for an explanation).
Uniform lump sum transfer to all households, with targeting energy-efficiency investments [b]	• Comparatively lower administrative costs per family to implement and administer • Provides an incentive to make energy-efficiency investments • Could alleviate relative poverty • May increase consumer purchases and overall consumption patterns	• Households that do not need support benefit from untargeted subsidy • Despite lower administrative costs per family, involves an additional layer of bureaucracy to oversee payments and ensure that funds are used for energy-efficiency investments • Payment per family likely to be small due to national budget constraints • Could increase energy and electricity consumption of households, for example in households that previously did not own a washing machine and as a result of the programme purchase an energy-efficient appliance for that purpose	**Non-seasonal, lump sum payments targeted at energy-efficiency measures are not modelled.** As above.
Income-tested cash transfer to vulnerable households, without targeting energy-efficiency investments [c]	• Households that need support benefit from targeted subsidy • Could alleviate extreme poverty • May increase consumer purchases and overall consumption patterns	• Relatively higher administrative costs to administer the scheme, unless existing definition of vulnerable households is used and this measure is added to an existing poverty relief programme • Without designation for gas, heating and electricity payments, no incentive to implement energy-saving measures, such as thermal modernisation or replacement of heating sources (although increased consumption may result in replacement of inefficient appliances) • Payment per family likely to be small due to national budget constraints • Does not include a mix of policy instruments (identifying poor people, providing incentives for energy efficiency investments) and does not ensure that the source of vulnerability to energy poverty is addressed • Depending on the size of payments, may entail a disincentive to work	**Cash transfers could be seasonal (as in the United Kingdom).** **Lump sum payments are modelled.** Currently, an ineffective way (cost per person too high) to provide relief to at-risk families. Energy and electricity sectors in Moldova currently do not meet preconditions for this kind of monetisation (see description of measures in other countries for an explanation). Modelling shows this to be an ineffective way to alleviate energy poverty.

Table 4.2. **Financial and investment measures** (continued)

Measure	Advantages	Disadvantages	Conclusion
Income-tested cash transfer to vulnerable households, with targeting energy-efficiency investments [d]	• Households that need support benefit from targeted transfer • Provides incentive to make energy-efficiency investments • Could alleviate relative poverty • May increase consumer purchases and overall consumption patterns	• Relatively higher administrative costs to administer the scheme, unless existing definition of vulnerable households is used and the measure is added to an existing poverty relief programme • Despite lower administrative costs per family, involves an additional layer of bureaucracy to oversee payments and ensure that funds are used for energy efficiency investments • Payment per family likely to be small, due to national budget constraints • Could increase energy and electricity consumption of households, for example in households that previously did not own a washing machine and as a result of the programme purchase an energy-efficient appliance for that purpose	Not modelled
VAT compensation/ rebate, for low-income/ vulnerable households	• Low-income and vulnerable households protected from tax increases for selected utility services (e.g. electricity, district heating, gas)	• Addresses vulnerability issues, but does not address sources of vulnerability (no curative measures) • No incentive for investment in energy efficiency • May lead to an increase in energy consumption	**Incremental VAT modelled for low-income households (difference between current VAT rate and proposed increase) for district heating, gas and electricity** **Two different definitions of low-income and vulnerable households are proposed (x% of spending on energy or any particular income).**
0% / 8% VAT rate for low-income/vulnerable households	• Low-income and vulnerable households protected from tax increases for selected utility services (e.g. electricity, district heating, gas)	• Addresses vulnerability issues but does not address the sources of vulnerability (no curative measures) • No incentive for investment in energy efficiency • May lead to an increase in energy consumption • Significant impact on the national budget	**0%/8% VAT rate modelled for low-income households for district heating, gas and electricity** **Two different definitions of low-income and vulnerable households are proposed (x% of spending on energy or particular income).**
Variable % VAT rate, for low-income / vulnerable households	• Low-income and vulnerable households protected from tax increases for selected utility services (e.g. electricity, district heating, gas) for a basic / minimum level of consumption • Small incentive for investment in energy efficiency	• Addresses vulnerability issues but does not address the sources of vulnerability (no curative measures) • Small incentive for investment in energy efficiency but few means to make these investments • May lead to an increase in energy consumption • Significant impact on the national budget	Not modelled
Retrofit investment programme, non-targeted	• Addresses curative measures (reduces energy consumption and impact of energy poverty) • Addresses other policy objectives related to energy efficiency and climate change	• High administrative costs related to identifying, implementing, and monitoring the impact of energy efficiency investments • Does not provide relief for low-income households (energy consumption may decrease, but households may still need support to pay bills)	Not modelled The creation of a retrofit programme requires a separate model and policy framework. That said, such programmes should be included in any policy mix.

Table 4.2. **Financial and investment measures** *(continued)*

Measure	Advantages	Disadvantages	Conclusion
Retrofit investment programme, targeted at low-income/ vulnerable households	• Addresses curative measures (reduces energy consumption and impact of energy poverty)	• High administrative costs related to identifying, implementing and monitoring the impact of energy-efficiency investments, as well as identifying vulnerable households • Does not provide relief for low-income households (energy consumption may decrease, but households may still need support to pay bills)	As above
Appliance grant programme, non-targeted	• Addresses curative measures (reduces energy consumption and impact of energy poverty) • Addresses other policy objectives related to energy efficiency and climate change	• Medium-high administrative costs related to identifying, implementing, and monitoring the impact of investments in efficient appliances • Does not provide relief for low-income households (electricity consumption may decrease, but households may still need support to pay bills)	As above
Appliance grant programme, targeted at low-income/ vulnerable households	• Addresses curative measures (reduces energy consumption and impact of energy poverty)	• Medium-high administrative costs related to identifying, implementing, and monitoring the impact of investments in efficient appliances as well as identifying vulnerable households • Does not provide relief for low-income households (electricity consumption may decrease, but households may still need support to pay bills)	As above

Notes: a. In addition, these types of payments can be divided into seasonal and non-seasonal. The description here refers to non-seasonal (that is, the payment occurs regardless of the season, such as on a monthly basis). For seasonal payments (for example, a winter fuel payment or a cold weather payment), the main advantage is that more funds will be available overall, as the support is targeted to address a specific time period. Further, seasonal payments increase the likelihood that support will go towards meeting increased heating costs. The main disadvantage of seasonal payments is that additional administrative costs will be necessary to oversee the support programme.

b. See previous note. On the other hand, seasonal payments would make it difficult to undertake energy-efficiency investments, many of which would need to take place outside the winter season.

c. For lump-sum, non-income-tested transfers: seasonal and non-seasonal payments are considered.

d. See previous note. On the other hand, seasonal payments would make it difficult to undertake energy-efficiency investments, many of which would need to take place outside the winter season.

4.4. Conclusions

On the basis of the above discussion, the following six compensation scenarios were identified for further analysis:

- **Scenario 0:** No compensation for poor households
- **Scenario 1:** Income-tested ($x\%$ rule), VAT compensation in cash
- **Scenario 2:** Income-tested ($x\%$ rule), VAT compensation in voucher
- **Scenario 3:** Income-tested ($x\%$ rule), compensation in cash over $y\%$ of energy spending in disposable household income
- **Scenario 4:** MDL 4 000 poverty definition, lump-sum compensation in cash
- **Scenario 5:** MDL 4 000 poverty definition, VAT compensation with voucher.

These scenarios are discussed further and more explanation is provided in the next chapter. Chapter 5 presents the results from the modelling of the impacts of the reform of the VAT rate on electricity, natural gas and heat, in relation to each of these scenarios, are analysed in detail.

Notes

1. Income-testing, or means-testing, is a process used to qualify for some benefits. Benefit payments go to those persons or households that can demonstrate that their income (for all sources, including other benefits, if applicable) and capital are below specified limits. It requires high levels of administrative costs to track income levels and monitor whether limits are appropriate. The classic example is the United Kingdom, where households report their income from all sources, including benefits, their age, household status (marital status, number of persons per household, type of household), place of residence, and other factors, to determine if they qualify for benefits. These benefits can be applied for and calculated online. See https://www.gov.uk/winter-fuel-payment/overview.

2. This 50% reduction is an arbitrary number, but it is suggested because reducing household extreme poverty by half is a realistic objective for any such social measure.

3. *Idem.*

4. *Idem.*

5. *Idem.*

References

Municipal Council of the City of Chisinau (2016), *Municipal Council Decision "Cu privire la acordarea de compensații pentru plata resurselor energetice persoanelor defavorizate social din municipal Chișinău în sezonul de încălzire 2016-2017"* (Concerning the granting of compensation for the payment of energy resources to the socially disadvantaged people in Chisinau Municipality during the heating season 2016-2017), www.chisinau.md/public/files/anul_2016/cmcsedinte/24.11.2016/14.compensatii_resurse_energetice_2016-2017.PDF.

Pye, S. et al. (2015), *Energy Poverty and Vulnerable Consumers in the Energy Sector across the EU: Analysis of Policies and Measures*, Insight_E, https://ec.europa.eu/energy/sites/ener/files/documents/INSIGHT_E_Energy%20Poverty%20-%20Main%20Report_FINAL.pdf.

Chapter 5

Modelling the impacts of energy subsidy reform in Moldova

This chapter introduces an Excel-based model designed to analyse the reform of the subsidy to households through a reduced value-added tax (VAT) rate on electricity, natural gas and heat. The chapter also discusses the social impact of the reform on poor households in relation to the six compensation scenarios identified earlier in the analysis, as well as the environmental and fiscal consequences of the reform.

5.1. Introduction to the model and compensation scenarios analysed

To analyse the impact of the reform of the selected subsidy schemes, an Excel-based spreadsheet was developed. This is a partial equilibrium model that measures the impact of reforms on energy affordability of different income groups and concurrently on greenhouse gas (GHG) emission levels and budgetary revenue and expenditure (net savings). The subsidy reform i.e. an increase of the value-added tax (VAT) rate up to the standard 20% rate on gas, electricity and heat, will have a direct impact on energy prices. This in turn will affect household consumption, expenditure and energy affordability. In general, the proposed model is illustrated in Figure 5.1.

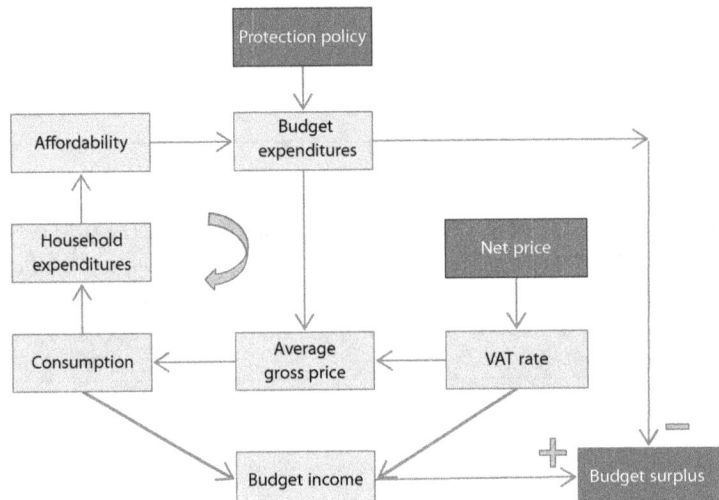

Figure 5.1. **Illustration of model algorithm**

The net price of the energy carrier is assumed to be stable. This is a simplification, because general equilibrium theory assumes that the supply side responds to decreased consumption by adjusting the price. The simplification is justified because of the relatively small changes in the final consumption and the situation of energy suppliers in Moldova, who generally generate losses and thus cannot decrease the price. Further explanation of the partial equilibrium model is provided in Box 5.1.

Box 5.1. **Explanation of the partial equilibrium model**

A partial equilibrium model is a simple supply and demand model of a single market. It consists of two equations, supply and demand, and two variables, price and quantity.

On the supply side, the response to an increase in demand is a lower price. Similarly, the response to a decrease in demand would be a higher price. On the consumer side, the response is the opposite: a higher price implies lower demand and a lower price implies higher demand.

Box 5.1. **Explanation of the partial equilibrium model** *(continued)*

In order to formulate the problem, a simple function for consumers is proposed:
Q >= iQ + dQ*P, iQ > 0 and dQ < 0 and P > 0
Where:
P is the price for the energy carrier
Q is the quantity of energy consumed
iQ is the intercept of demand on the Q axis (demand at P = 0)
dQ is the response of demand to changes in price (in other words 1/price elasticity)

The two proposed functions intersect at a point of the current demand and the current price, as illustrated in Figure 5.2 (S – Supply, D – Demand).

Figure 5.2. **Illustration of a partial equilibrium model**

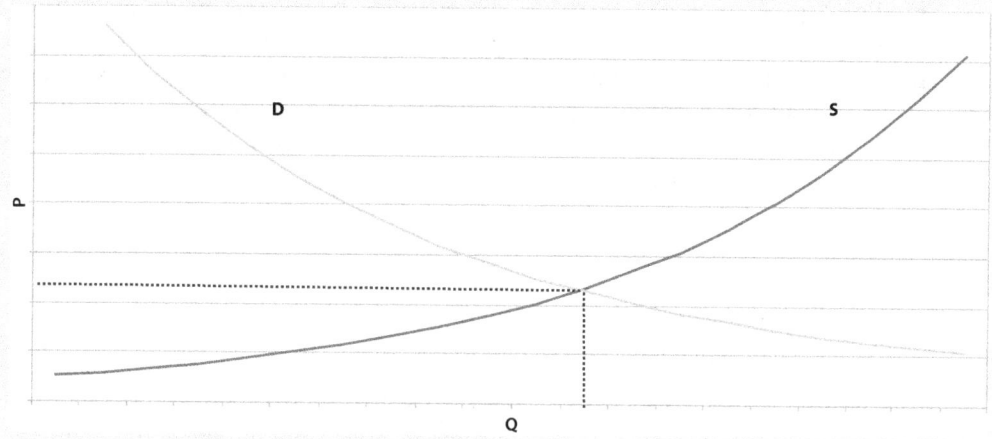

Before increasing the VAT tax equilibrium, the producer price (lower VAT) equals the consumer price. This is illustrated on Figure 5.3 by point A. The increase of the VAT tax rate to 20% would cause a reduction in the quantity of energy carrier traded. This is illustrated by the new S curve. Both the supplier and the consumer price would fall, i.e. the tax burden would be shared between the parties. The new equilibrium point B would be reached, resulting in a decrease in energy carrier demand and a decrease in the net price (and an increase in the gross, end-user, price).

Figure 5.3. **Illustration of a price increase in a partial equilibrium model**

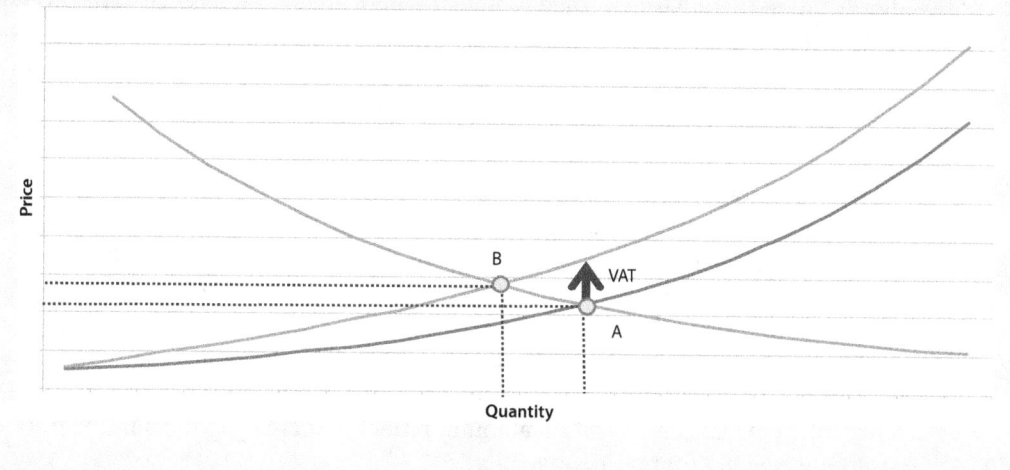

The proposed simplified method assumes that consumers will respond to a price increase (consumption will fall), but the producer will not respond. Thus, the new price is simply the old price + an increased VAT.

The model also tests the proposed policy options for protecting poor households. The policy options for protecting poor households are tested together with the impact of the reform on energy consumption and, indirectly, on budget revenue and expenditure.

The following scenarios to protect poor households, tested in this analysis, are:

1. **Scenario 0:** No compensation for poor households. This is a baseline simulation presenting what would happen if VAT on energy carriers is increased, and no policy to protect poor households is established. The basic outcome of this simulation is a price increase, decrease in consumption, and an increase in the burden of energy costs.

2. **Scenario 1:** Income-tested ($x\%$ rule), VAT compensation in cash. This scenario implies a protection measure that compensates poor households for the VAT increase (understood as the difference between the amount spent before and after the VAT increase, taking into account changes in consumption). This measure will concern households that spend more than $x\%$ of their disposable income on a particular energy carrier. The proposed share of disposable household income spent is different for each energy carrier:

   - 6% for electricity
   - 3% for natural gas used for cooking
   - 10% for natural gas used for cooking and for heating
   - 15% for centrally supplied heating.

   The proposed percentages are a compromise between lessons learnt from other countries and the realistic costs of the compensation (making the entire population eligible for compensation is not effective). However, these compensation shares can be further adjusted should the government of Moldova think it necessary.

3. **Scenario 2:** Income-tested ($x\%$ rule), VAT compensation in vouchers. This scenario is similar to the previous one, the difference being that instead of paying compensation in cash, it is paid by voucher, which authorises the energy supplier to use a lower VAT. This solution decreases the administrative costs of distributing the compensation. The voucher system can work as follows: once a year, the responsible authority of the Ministry of Health, Labour and Social Protection performs an income test and a test on household's spending on a particular energy carrier and issues a voucher that entitles the household to a VAT exemption from the energy provider. The voucher is delivered to the energy provider that issues invoices without VAT for entitled families.[1]

4. **Scenario 3:** Income-tested ($x\%$ rule), compensation over $x\%$ in cash. This option takes into account not only the increase of VAT but also energy poverty, in general. It implies that all households that spend more than $x\%$ of their disposable income on a given energy carrier are entitled to receive compensation in cash. The amount of the compensation is the difference between actual spending and the amount that would be spent, not exceeding $x\%$ of disposable household income. Obviously, this scenario will require an effort to collect income and expenditure data and to calculate the correct compensation amount, probably increasing the administrative costs for the social programme manager.

5. **Scenario 4:** MDL 4 000 poverty definition, lump sum in cash. With this option, households with disposable income lower than a given amount are entitled to a lump-sum compensation. The lump sum is calculated as the difference in spending before and after the VAT increase for a given energy carrier for a median-income family. The income test could be performed once per year, while lump sum is paid on a monthly basis.

   The proposed amount of MDL 4 000 per month is the authors' assumption. This amount reflects the level of income above which consumers can afford to pay their energy bills without receiving compensation. The amount was chosen to correlate with the compensation levels defined in other scenarios, especially with Scenario 1. This correlation implies that it is more or less the same group of the population that will be compensated by the VAT increase in this and other scenarios.

6. **Scenario 5:** MDL 4 000 poverty definition, VAT compensation in vouchers. The disposable income rule is used as above, but instead of paying compensation as a lump sum, it is paid by voucher, which authorises the energy supplier to use a lower VAT. As in Scenario 2, the voucher system can work as follows: once a year, the responsible authority of the Ministry of Health, Labour and Social Protection performs an income test and issues a voucher that entitles the household to a VAT exemption from the energy provider. The voucher is delivered to the energy provider that issues invoices without VAT for entitled families.[2]

The model also includes several key assumptions that are described further here. These include assumptions on household income, income distribution and family size, energy consumption, price elasticity of demand, administrative costs of the compensation distribution and CO_2 emission levels.

5.1.1. Assumptions on household income, distribution and family size

Income distribution

Instead of testing the average or median disposable household income, the model takes into account the distribution of income per capita as provided by the National Bureau of Statistics of Moldova.

Table 5.1. **Distribution of disposable household income per capita, %**

Disposable income distribution	Urban	Rural
	%	
Total	100.0	100.0
Of which, average monthly disposable income per capita, in MDL:		
up to 200	0.9	3.0
200.1-400.0	0.7	4.9
400.1-600.0	1.9	6.6
600.1-800.0	2.2	10.4
800.1-1 000.0	4.6	12.4
1 000.1-1 200.0	5.8	11.5
1 200.1-1 400.0	9.4	11.2
1 400.1-1 600.0	8.9	8.3

Table 5.1. **Distribution of disposable household income per capita, %** *(continued)*

Disposable income distribution	Urban	Rural
	%	
1 600.1-1 800.0	8.3	5.3
1 800.1-2 000.0	7.4	4.9
2 000.1-2 200.0	7.5	4.1
2 200.1-2 400.0	5.8	3.4
2 400.1-2 600.0	5.8	2.5
2 600.1-2 800.0	4.2	2.2
2 800.1-3 000.0	3.6	1.2
3 000.1 and over	22.8	8.1

Source: National Bureau of Statistics of Moldova. www.statistica.md/index.php?l=en. Accessed in April 2017.

As there are significant differences between urban and rural areas, all calculations in the model were divided into the following categories: city of Chisinau, city of Balti (which also has district heating), other towns and rural areas. For each, a different distribution of disposable household income and family size was used.

Average household size

Table 5.2. **Average size of households, number of people**

	2016
Average	2.3
Urban	2.3
Rural	2.4
Big cities (Chisinau and Balti)	2.3
Small cities	2.3

Source: National Bureau of Statistics of Moldova. www.statistica.md/index.php?l=en. Accessed in April 2017.

The average size of a household in Moldova is estimated to consist of 2.3 people. This information is necessary and it is used in the model to convert consumption of energy by households into per capita consumption of energy.

5.1.2. *Assumptions for energy consumption*

Given that there are no specific data on the distribution of energy consumption across households in Moldova, the authors of this report needed to make a number of assumptions related to consumption levels across income groups (e.g. lowest level of consumption, highest level of consumption). These assumptions are based on the experience of other countries with the distribution of energy consumption across end users.

Electricity

The average electricity consumption of consumption in Moldova is 1 277.67 kWh per year, accounting for electricity consumption by households and the number of households connected. The model assumes that this amount is consumed by households with incomes of about MDL 3 700 per month. It is assumed, however, that poorer and richer families consume respectively less and more. The lowest consumption is assumed to be half of the average, while the highest consumption is assumed to increase up to 1 500 kWh per year.

Natural gas for cooking

Given that the consumption of natural gas for cooking is usually small, on average, it is below 30 m³ per month, the legislation allows for the gas for cooking to be priced at a lower tariff. The annual consumption of gas in this case was assumed to be 2 027.34 kWh, corresponding to consumption of 15 m³ of natural gas per month. The model assumes that this amount is consumed by households with income of about MDL 3 700 per month. It is assumed, however, that poorer and richer families consume respectively less and more. The lowest consumption is assumed to be half of the average, while the highest consumption is set at 2 382.12 kWh per year.

Natural gas for cooking and heating

It is assumed that the consumption of natural gas for cooking and heating is above 30 m³ per month, thus the price for this combined consumption is higher. The annual combined consumption was assumed to be 8 109.36 kWh, corresponding to the consumption of 60 m³ of natural gas per month (average during the year). While this value is higher than in many other countries, it is important to note that most homes in Moldova are poorly insulated, which explains this high consumption. The model assumes that this amount is consumed by households with income of about MDL 3 700 per month. It is assumed, however, that poorer and richer families consume respectively less and more. The lowest consumption is assumed to be half of the average, while the highest is set at 9 528.50 kWh per year.

Heating

Heat energy consumption was assumed to be 8 250 kWh, corresponding to the annual consumption of 150 kWh per square metre for an apartment of 55 m². This value is higher than in many other countries. This is explained by the fact that most of the homes in Moldova are poorly insulated, which leads to a higher consumption of heat. The model assumes that this amount is consumed by households with income of about MDL 3 700 per month. Poorer and richer families consume respectively less and more. The lowest consumption is assumed to be half of the average, while the highest is set at 9 693.75 kWh per year.

Assumptions for the change in energy consumption – price elasticity of demand

The key parameter used to assess the change of consumer demand as a result of the change of price of a given good or service is price elasticity of demand. Price elasticity shows how the demand for energy (or the consumption of electricity, gas and heat) will change as a result of the price increase of energy. To estimate the change in consumption (which is a decrease) and based on other similar analyses, price elasticity for natural gas and heating of -0.113 was used.[3] Similarly, for electricity, price elasticity of -0.111 was used. A relatively low elasticity of demand (below 1) implies that people do not really have options to switch to other sources of energy and continue to use available sources, despite the increase of price. One way to save on energy costs is by reducing thermal comfort in homes, but such savings will not be significant and this is not a socially advisable option.

While the choice of elasticities for Moldova may see seem rather low, particularly compared to other low-income countries, it should be noted that the starting conditions in Moldova are somewhat different. First, Moldovan households have very high energy costs compared to their income. While high elasticity of energy demand was observed at the beginning of the price increase in the 1990s, there is now very little room for adjusting energy use. Much higher elasticities are usually reported for countries that see a steep increase of energy prices – going from low to high prices. Second, the choice of elasticity impacts the calculations of higher-income households only. As low-income households are expected to receive compensation anyway, this implies no change in demand across this group of households. At the same time, higher-income households usually have lower elasticities of demand. In this case, and given the specific Moldovan circumstances, a relatively lower elasticity of demand, closer to the elasticity of demand of higher-income households chosen for this analysis, is deemed more relevant.

Administrative costs of distribution of the compensation

The distribution of the compensation for the VAT increase will entail administrative costs. Based on similar programmes in other countries, it can be estimated that up to 2% of the compensation must be spent on programme administration. For example, a programme in Poland to distribute social aid to 3.8 million families required the employment of 7 000 people, or 0.001842105 working places per household receiving the aid. This indicator was used to estimate the administrative costs in Moldova, assuming an average monthly salary for administrative employees of MDL 6 144.2 (according to the National Bureau of Statistics) and 50% of overhead (social security and other administrative costs to organise and transfer social aid). This gives an annual cost of MDL 203.73 per household receiving aid for energy costs.

If the support programme uses vouchers, it is assumed that the administrative work would be significantly less time-consuming, and the costs are estimated to be one-twelfth of the distribution of aid in cash. Vouchers will entail less administration, due to the fact that they are normally checked and distributed once a year, while the fiscal control of electricity/gas/heat energy distributors is far more intensive. In case of a lump sum in cash, it is assumed that administrative costs would be smaller by half, due to the fact that it will not be necessary to monitor individual energy bills, and the same amount of aid will be distributed to all beneficiaries.

Unit CO_2 emissions

The unit emission of 0.41205 kg of CO_2 per kWh (DEFRA, 2016) of energy delivered by the grid was used to estimate CO_2 emissions before and after introducing the reform. The same indicator was used for heating. For natural gas, the indicator of 0.18404 kg of CO_2 per kWh (Carbon Trust, 2013) was used to estimate CO_2 emissions before and after introducing the reform.

5.2. Results of the modelling

The model calculates reform impacts separately for each energy carrier and urbanisation type as follows:

- electricity (Chisinau, Balti, towns, rural areas)
- natural gas used for cooking (Chisinau, Balti, towns, rural areas)

- natural gas used for cooking and heating (Chisinau, Balti, towns, rural areas)
- heating (Chisinau, Balti).

Although the standard VAT rate in Moldova is 20%, this reform might not be implemented immediately. In this case, it is reasonable to consider some intermediate solutions through a step-wise increase. One possible option is to increase VAT for electricity and heating to a reduced VAT rate of 8%. For the sake of comparison, the results of modelling for a 5% reduced VAT rate are also provided.

5.2.1. Electricity

The model simulations show the impact that an increase in the VAT rate would have on the end-user price for electricity, electricity consumption, and GHG emissions. The model results provide insights not only into the impact of the VAT rate increase on the economy as a whole and the public budget, but also in terms of social impact.

Impact on end-user price

The gross average end-user price would increase from MDL 2.0352 to MDL 2.4422 per kWh. This is an increase of 20% over the current value.

From Figure 5.4, it is clear that most of the price change would result in an increase in the price for households.

Figure 5.4. **Impact of subsidy reform in the electricity sector on end-user price, in MDL**

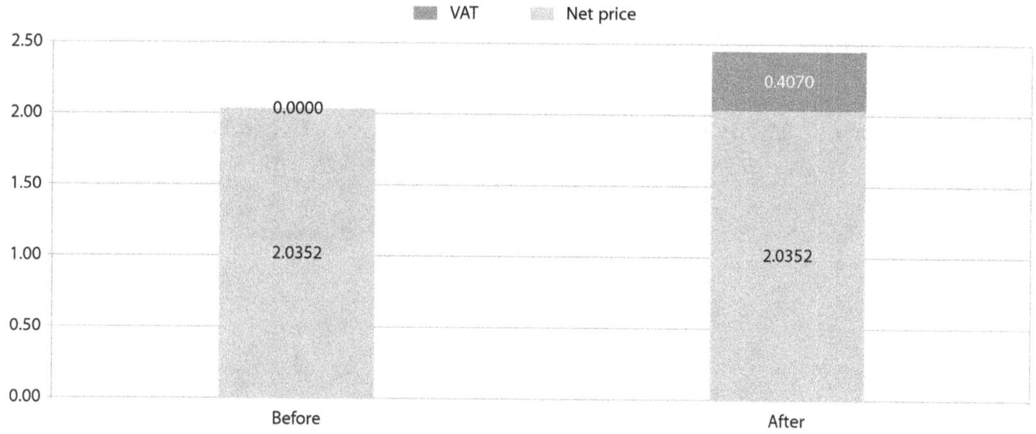

	VAT	Net price
Before	0.0000	2.0352
After	0.4070	2.0352

Source: Authors' own calculations based on the model.

Impact on electricity consumption

If no protection policy is introduced, electricity consumption would fall by about 3%. If a compensation policy is introduced, the drop in electricity consumption would still be visible, but would amount to only about 1%. This small decrease will be triggered mostly by a decrease in consumption by wealthier households, since poor families will not change their consumption, due to the compensation they will receive.

Impact on GHG emissions

The GHG emissions associated with the decrease in electricity consumption would not be significant: 1 179 tCO_2 annually. If a compensation policy is implemented, the decrease would be about 400 to 550 tonnes of CO_2 annually. If the protection measure compensates households not only for the VAT increase but covers all households that spend more than 6% of their disposable income on electricity, the decrease would be about 101 tonnes of CO_2 annually, due to an increase in consumption by poorer households.

Table 5.3 and Figure 5.5 illustrate the impact of VAT increase on GHG emissions under all scenarios.

Table 5.3. **Impact of subsidy reform in the electricity sector on GHG emissions under different scenarios, tCO_2 annually (VAT 20%)**

Scenario	No compensation	x% rule, VAT compensation in cash	x% rule, VAT compensation with voucher	x% rule, compensation over x% in cash	MDL 4 000, lump sum in cash	MDL 4 000, VAT compensation with voucher
CO_2 emissions from consumption at current price	53 110	53 110	53 110	53 110	53 110	53 110
CO_2 emissions from consumption at new price	51 931	51 931	51 931	51 931	51 931	51 931
CO_2 emissions from consumption at new price, with compensation	51 931	52 613	52 613	53 009	52 681	52 567
Decrease of CO_2 emissions	1 179	1 179	1 179	1 179	1 179	1 179
Decrease of CO_2 emissions, with compensation	1 179	497	497	101	429	542

Source: Authors' own calculations based on the model.

Figure 5.5. **Impact of subsidy reform in the electricity sector on GHG emissions for different scenarios, tCO_2 annually (VAT 20%)**

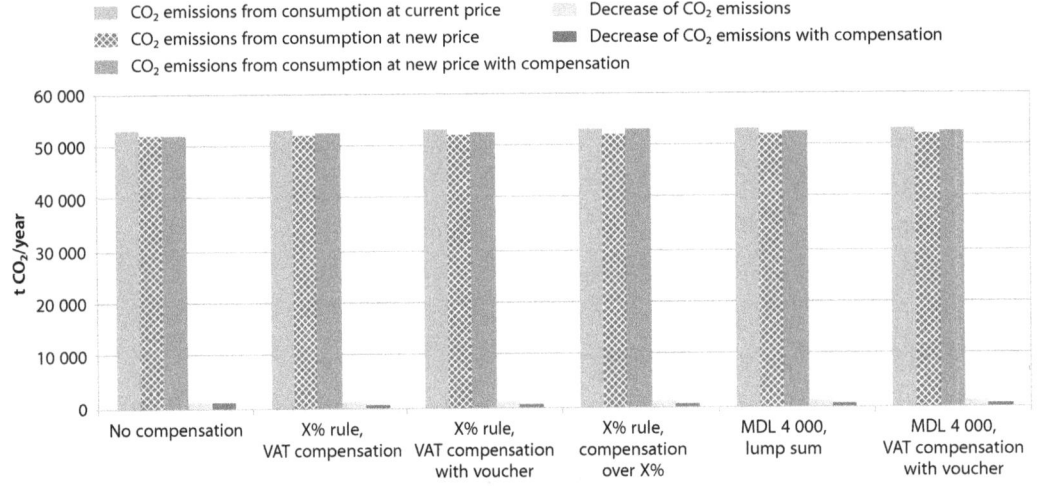

Source: Authors' own calculations based on the model.

Tables 5.4 and 5.5 present the impact of a reduced VAT increase on GHG emissions under all scenarios.

The GHG emissions associated with the decrease in electricity consumption would be: 482 tCO_2 annually for a 8% VAT and 295 tCO_2 annually for a 5% VAT. If a compensation policy is implemented, the decrease would be in the range of 174 to 232 tonnes of CO_2 annually for a 8% VAT and 111 to 142 tCO_2 annually for a 5% VAT. In case of "*x*% rule, compensation over *x*%" scenario, there will be an increase of the GHG emissions due to an increase in consumption by poorer households.

Table 5.4. **Impact of subsidy reform in the electricity sector on GHG emissions under different scenarios, tCO_2 annually (VAT 8%)**

Scenario	No compensation	*x*% rule, VAT compensation in cash	*x*% rule, VAT compensation with voucher	*x*% rule, compensation over *x*% in cash	MDL 4 000, lump sum in cash	MDL 4 000, VAT compensation with voucher
CO_2 emissions from consumption at current price	53 110	53 110	53 110	53 110	53 110	53 110
CO_2 emissions from consumption at new price	52 638	52 638	52 638	52 638	52 638	52 638
CO_2 emissions from consumption at new price, with compensation	52 638	52 877	52 877	53 359	52 935	52 889
Decrease of CO_2 emissions	472	472	472	472	472	472
Decrease of CO_2 emissions, with compensation	472	232	232	-250	174	221

Source: Authors' own calculations based on the model.

Table 5.5. **Impact of subsidy reform in the electricity sector on GHG emissions under different scenarios, tCO_2 annually (VAT 5%)**

Scenario	No compensation	*x*% rule, VAT compensation in cash	*x*% rule, VAT compensation with voucher	*x*% rule, compensation over *x*% in cash	MDL 4 000, lump sum in cash	MDL 4 000, VAT compensation with voucher
CO_2 emissions from consumption at current price	53 110	53 110	53 110	53 110	53 110	53 110
CO_2 emissions from consumption at new price	52 815	52 815	52 815	52 815	52 815	52 815
CO_2 emissions from consumption at new price, with compensation	52 815	52 967	52 967	53 453	52 999	52 972
Decrease of CO_2 emissions	295	295	295	295	295	295
Decrease of CO_2 emissions, with compensation	295	142	142	-343	111	138

Source: Authors' own calculations based on the model.

Impact on the public budget

The increase in the VAT rate on electricity consumption would lead to an increase in budget revenue. The budget revenue would increase by MDL 546 million annually. The costs of compensation would vary from MDL 296 million to MDL 521 million annually, depending on the compensation scenario. The administrative costs of the distribution of the compensation would be the highest in case of cash compensation and would amount to MDL 156 million annually. In case of a lump-sum cash distribution, the administrative costs would amount to MDL 69 million annually, while in the case of vouchers, it would decrease to MDL 11 million to MDL 12 million annually.

The budget surplus from reforming the subsidies would be significant, from MDL 112 million to MDL 283 million, except for *Scenario 3* ($x\%$ rule, compensation over $x\%$). In that case, there will be more expenditure than income to the budget. Table 5.6 and Figure 5.6 illustrate the VAT reform impact on the budget under each scenario.

Table 5.6. **Impact of subsidy reform in the electricity sector on the public budget under different scenarios, in MDL annually (VAT 20%)**

Scenario	No compensation	$x\%$ rule, VAT compensation in cash	$x\%$ rule, VAT compensation with voucher	$x\%$ rule, compensation over $x\%$ in cash	MDL 4 000, lump sum in cash	MDL 4 000, VAT compensation with voucher
Budget revenue	545 699 462	594 232 440	594 232 440	622 361 359	599 047 372	590 972 967
Compensation costs	0	-326 394 759	-326 394 759	-521 125 764	-353 097 393	-296 049 112
Administration costs	0	-155 717 780	-12 976 482	-155 717 780	-69 165 049	-11 527 508
Budget surplus	545 699 462	112 119 902	254 861 200	-54 482 185	176 784 930	283 396 347

Source: Authors' own calculations based on the model.

Figure 5.6. **Impact of subsidy reform in the electricity sector on public budget: budget income, expenditure and surplus for different scenarios, in MDL**

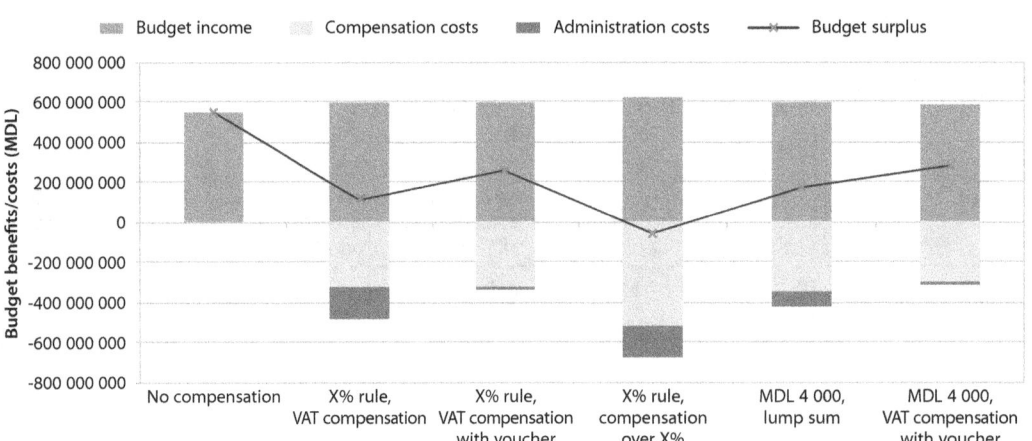

Source: Authors' own calculations based on the model.

Tables 5.7 and 5.8 below present the impact of a lower VAT increase on the public budget under all scenarios.

The budget revenue would increase by MDL 221 million annually if VAT is increased to 8% and MDL 139 million annually if VAT is increased to 5%. The costs of compensation would vary from MDL 114 million to MDL 356 million annually, depending on the compensation scenario, if VAT is increased to 8% and from MDL 73 million to MDL 317 million annually if VAT is increased to 5%.

The administrative costs of the distribution of the compensation would be the highest in case of cash compensation and would amount to MDL 138 million annually. In case of a lump-sum cash distribution, the administrative costs would amount to MDL 69 million annually while in the case of vouchers, it would decrease to MDL 11 million to MDL 12 million annually. The administrative costs are similar under the different VAT increase scenarios, because compensation will cover the same or almost the same group of households.

The budget surplus from reforming the subsidies would amount to MDL 108 million to MDL 111 million for the scenarios with compensation with vouchers and a VAT increase to 8% and MDL 63 to MDL 64 for a VAT increase to 5%. All other scenarios will generate a budget deficit.

Table 5.7. **Impact of subsidy reform in the electricity sector on the public budget under different scenarios, in MDL annually (VAT 8%)**

Scenario	No compensation	x% rule, VAT compensation in cash	x% rule, VAT compensation with voucher	x% rule, compensation over x% in cash	MDL 4 000, lump sum in cash	MDL 4 000, VAT compensation with voucher
Budget revenue	221 634 061	236 949 633	236 949 633	267 802 514	240 670 772	237 681 956
Compensation costs	0	-114 757 473	-114 757 473	-356 308 931	-141 238 957	-117 930 586
Administration costs	0	-138 330 099	-11 527 508	-138 330 099	-69 165 049	-11 527 508
Budget surplus	221 634 061	-16 137 939	110 664 652	-226 836 516	30 266 765	108 223 861

Source: Authors' own calculations based on the model.

Table 5.8. **Impact of subsidy reform in the electricity sector on the public budget under different scenarios, in MDL annually (VAT 5%)**

Scenario	No compensation	x% rule, VAT compensation in cash	x% rule, VAT compensation with voucher	x% rule, compensation over x% in cash	MDL 4 000, lump sum in cash	MDL 4 000, VAT compensation with voucher
Budget revenue	139 045 394	148 524 297	148 524 297	178 741 253	150 476 438	148 816 022
Compensation costs	0	-72 600 738	-72 600 738	-316 999 245	-88 274 348	-73 888 287
Administration costs	0	-138 330 099	-11 527 508	-138 330 099	-69 165 049	-11 527 508
Budget surplus	139 045 394	-62 406 540	64 396 051	-276 588 091	-6 962 960	63 400 227

Source: Authors' own calculations based on the model.

Social impact

The social impact of the VAT rate increase is significant. The increase in the end-user price would result in an increase in household spending on electricity. The average bill would increase from MDL 217 per month to MDL 254 per month, which is an increase of 17.34%. The share of the average bill in household income would increase from 6.0% to 7.0%. The compensation would decrease the share of the bill, depending on the proposed scenario. The VAT compensation (*Scenarios 1* and *2*) has a relatively limited impact on the share of electricity costs in disposable household income of vulnerable families. This is so because the compensation package provided raises the income for such families to what it would have been before the VAT increase.

If a lump-sum payment is provided, the poorest families will enjoy a higher reduction in electricity costs as a share of disposable income. The best situation for vulnerable families can be observed under *Scenario 3* (x% rule, compensation over x%), where the compensation is calculated to keep the share of the costs at a level that does not exceed 6% of disposable household income. The results of this analysis are presented in Table 5.9 and Figure 5.7.

Table 5.9. **Social impact of subsidy reform: percentage of electricity costs in disposable household income under different scenarios (VAT 20%)**

Household income per capita	Scenario						
	Current price	No compensation	x% rule, VAT compensation in cash	x% rule, VAT compensation with voucher	x% rule, compensation over x% in cash	MDL 4 000, lump sum in cash	MDL 4 000, VAT compensation with voucher
0-200	24.0%	28.2%	24.0%	24.0%	6.0%	19.8%	24.0%
200-400	13.7%	16.1%	13.3%	13.3%	4.7%	11.3%	13.3%
400-600	10.3%	12.1%	10.0%	10.0%	6.0%	8.9%	10.0%
600-800	8.6%	10.1%	8.3%	8.3%	6.0%	7.7%	8.3%
800-1 000	7.5%	8.9%	7.3%	7.3%	6.0%	6.9%	7.3%
1 000-1 200	6.9%	8.0%	6.6%	6.6%	6.0%	6.4%	6.6%
1 200-1 400	6.4%	7.5%	6.2%	6.2%	5.8%	6.1%	6.2%
1 400-1 600	6.0%	7.0%	6.0%	6.0%	6.0%	5.8%	5.8%
1 600-1 800	5.3%	6.2%	5.3%	5.3%	6.0%	6.2%	6.2%
1 800-2 000	4.9%	5.8%	5.8%	5.8%	5.8%	5.8%	5.8%
2 000-2 200	4.6%	5.4%	5.4%	5.4%	5.4%	5.4%	5.4%
2 200-2 400	4.3%	5.0%	5.0%	5.0%	5.0%	5.0%	5.0%
2 400-2 600	4.0%	4.7%	4.7%	4.7%	4.7%	4.7%	4.7%
2 600-2 800	3.8%	4.5%	4.5%	4.5%	4.5%	4.5%	4.5%
2 800-3 000	3.7%	4.3%	4.3%	4.3%	4.3%	4.3%	4.3%
3 000-	3.5%	4.1%	4.1%	4.1%	4.1%	4.1%	4.1%

Source: Authors' own calculations based on the model.

Figure 5.7. **Social impact of subsidy reform: percentage of spending on electricity in household disposable budgets for different scenarios, %**

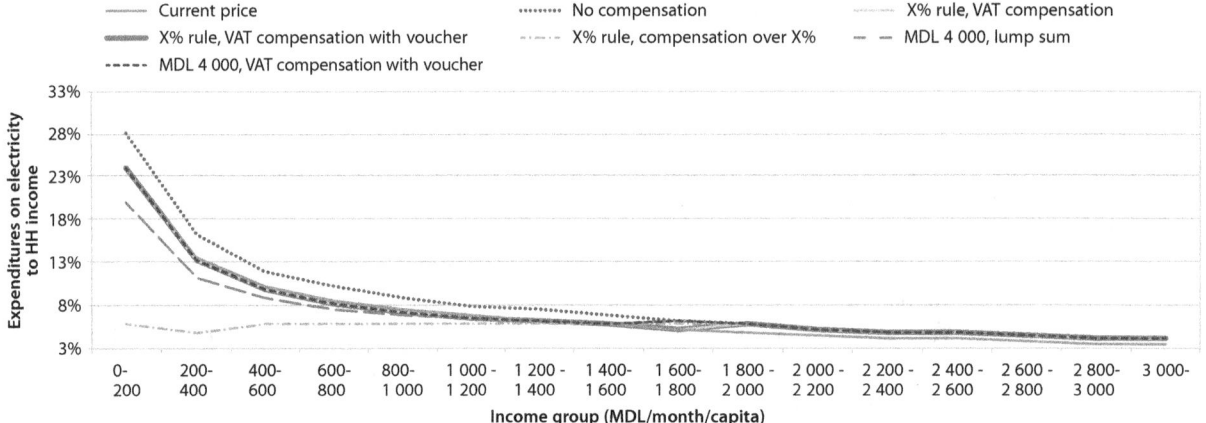

Source: Authors' own calculations based on the model.

Tables 5.10 and 5.11 below show the impact of a reduced VAT increase on the share of electricity costs in disposable household income under different scenarios. This comparison is done for households income per capita of MDL 1 600 to MDL 1 800 per month. This range was chosen because it is the median income in Chisinau and Balti. The results are similar irrespective of the VAT increase (an increase of the share of electricity costs in disposable household scenario of 5.3% to 5.7%) except for the no-compensation scenario. This is so because the increase of the VAT is compensated for by the protection measures.

Table 5.10. **Social impact of subsidy reform: percentage of electricity costs in disposable household income under different scenarios (VAT 8%)**

Household income per capita	Scenario						
	Current price	No compensation	x% rule, VAT compensation in cash	x% rule, VAT compensa-tion with voucher	x% rule, compensation over x% in cash	MDL 4 000, lump sum in cash	MDL 4 000, VAT compensation with voucher
MDL 1 600-1 800	5.3%	5.7%	5.7%	5.7%	5.7%	5.7%	5.7%

Source: Authors' own calculations based on the model.

Table 5.11. **Social impact of subsidy reform: percentage of electricity costs in disposable household income under different scenarios (VAT 5%)**

Household income per capita	Scenario						
	Current price	No compensation	x% rule, VAT compensation in cash	x% rule, VAT compensa-tion with voucher	x% rule, compensation over x% in cash	MDL 4 000, lump sum in cash	MDL 4 000, VAT compensation with voucher
MDL 1 600-1 800	5.3%	5.5%	5.5%	5.5%	5.5%	5.5%	5.5%

Source: Authors' own calculations based on the model.

5.2.2. *Natural gas*

The model simulations show the impact of the VAT rate increase on the end-user price for natural gas, natural gas consumption and GHG emissions. The model results also provide some insights on the impact the VAT rate increase would have on the economy, the public budget and on household budgets.

Impact on end-user price

The gross average end-user price would increase from MDL 0.5714 to MDL 0.6349 per kWh when using natural gas for cooking purposes only (monthly consumption of below 30 m^3).

Figure 5.8. **Impact of subsidy reform on end-user price for natural gas for cooking, in MDL**

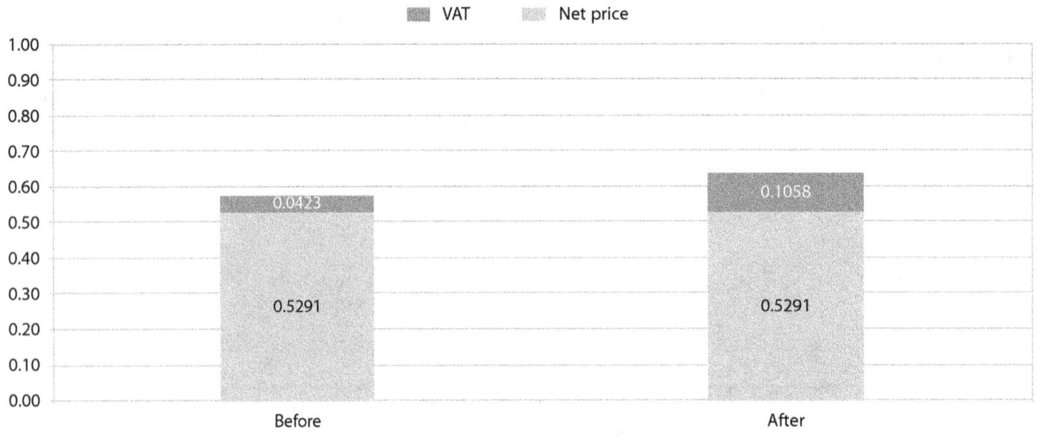

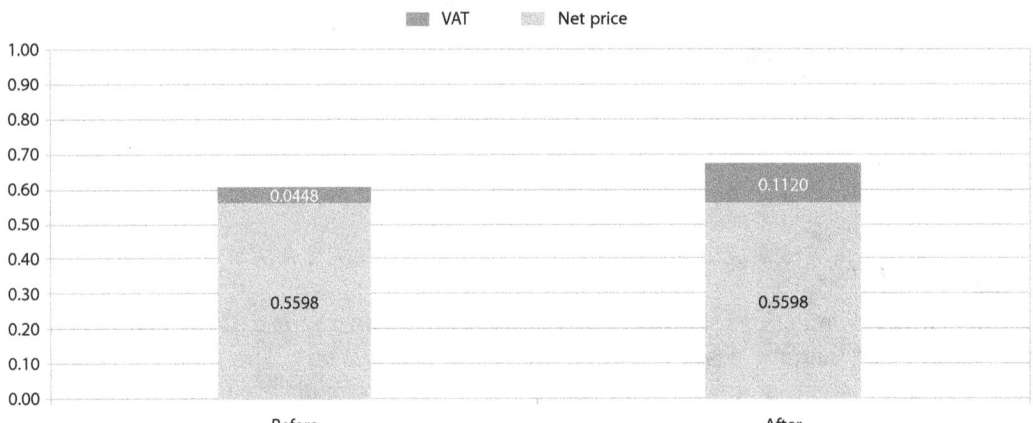

Source: Authors' own calculations based on the model.

The gross end-user price would increase from MDL 0.6046 to MDL 0.6718 per kWh when using natural gas for both cooking and heating purposes (monthly consumption of above 30 m^3).

Figure 5.9. **Impact of subsidy reform on end-user price for natural gas for cooking and heating, in MDL**

Source: Authors' own calculations based on the model.

Impact on consumption

If no compensation policy is implemented, natural gas consumption would decrease by about 1.3%. If a compensation policy is introduced, the decrease in natural gas consumption is still visible, but would amount to less than 1%, mostly due to the decrease in consumption by wealthier households. Poor households will not change their consumption levels, given to the compensation package they would receive.

Impact on GHG emissions

The GHG emissions associated with the decrease in natural gas consumption would not be significant: 1 236 Mg annually. If a compensation policy is implemented, the decrease would be about 500 to 600 tonnes of CO_2 annually. If the protection measure compensates households not only for the VAT increase but also covers all households that spend more than 3% of their disposable income (10% in case cooking and heating are considered together), GHG emissions would increase by about 516 tonnes of CO_2 annually, due to an increase in consumption by poorer households.

Table 5.12 and Figure 5.10 illustrate the impact of the reform on GHG emissions under all scenarios.

Table 5.12. **Impact of subsidy reform in the gas sector on GHG emissions under different scenarios, tCO_2 annually**

Scenario	No compensation	x% rule, VAT compensation in cash	x% rule, VAT compensation with voucher	x% rule, compensation over x% in cash	MDL 4 000, lump sum in cash	MDL 4 000, VAT compensation with voucher
CO_2 emissions from consumption at current price	99 790	99 790	99 790	99 790	99 790	99 790
CO_2 emissions from consumption at new price	98 554	98 554	98 554	98 554	98 554	98 554
CO_2 emissions from consumption at new price, with compensation	98 554	99 202	99 202	100 306	99 255	99 148
Decrease of CO_2 emissions	1 236	1 236	1 236	1 236	1 236	1 236
Decrease of CO_2 emissions, with compensation	1 236	588	588	-516	535	642

Source: Authors' own calculations based on the model.

Figure 5.10. **Impact of subsidy reform in the gas sector on GHG emissions for different scenarios, tCO_2 annually**

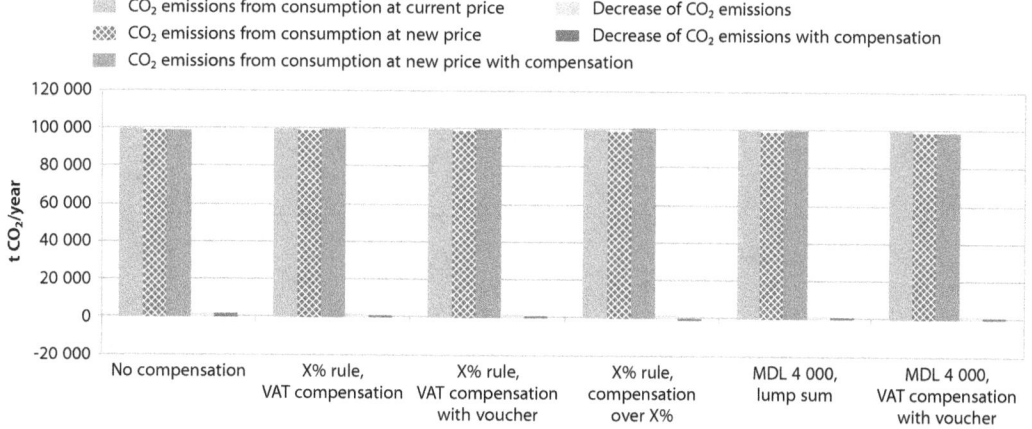

Source: Authors' own calculations based on the model.

Impact on the public budget

The increase of the VAT rate on natural gas consumption would lead to an increase in budget revenue. The budget revenue would increase by MDL 222 million annually. The costs of the compensation would vary from MDL 100 million to MDL 301 million annually depending on the compensation scenario. The administrative costs of the distribution of the compensation would be the highest in the case of cash compensation and would amount to MDL 66 million annually.

In case of a lump-sum cash distribution, the administrative costs would amount to MDL 31 million annually, while in the case of vouchers, they would amount to MDL 5 million annually.

In all cases, except one, the budget surplus resulting from the VAT increase on natural gas will range from MDL 63 million to MDL 131 million. In one case (*Scenario 3*) there will be more costs than revenue to the budget. Table 5.13 and Figure 5.11 illustrate the impact on the budget under all scenarios.

Table 5.13. **Impact of subsidy reform in the gas sector on the public budget under different scenarios, in MDL annually**

Scenario	No compensation	x% rule, VAT compensation in cash	x% rule, VAT compensation with voucher	x% rule, compensation over x% in cash	MDL 4 000, lump sum in cash	MDL 4 000, VAT compensation with voucher
Budget income	222 107 322	237 651 104	237 651 104	262 774 386	238 605 514	236 214 929
Compensation costs	0	-111 032 762	-111 032 762	-300 837 781	-117 746 352	-100 018 799
Administration costs	0	-63 255 290	-5 271 274	-66 057 117	-30 851 667	-5 141 945
Budget surplus	222 107 322	63 363 051	121 347 067	-104 120 512	90 007 495	131 054 185

Source: Authors' own calculations based on the model.

Figure 5.11. **Impact of subsidy reform in the gas sector on the public budget – income, expenditure and surplus from the reform for different scenarios, in MDL**

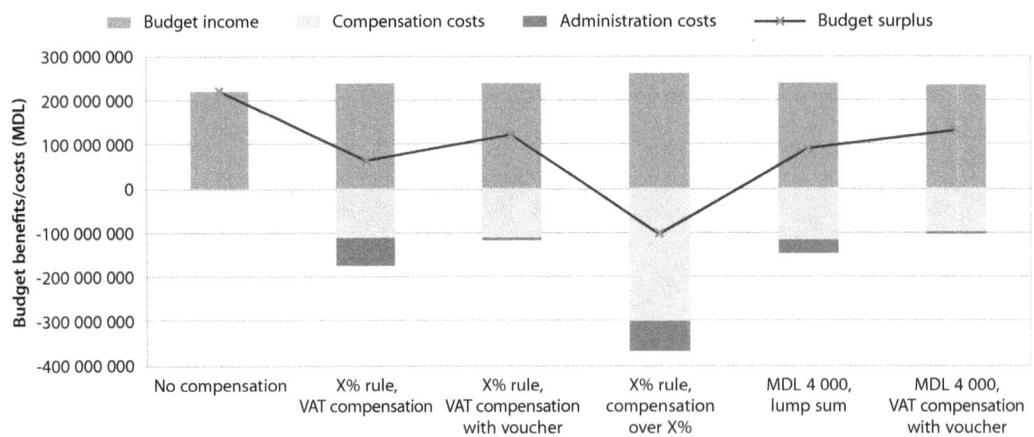

Source: Authors' own calculations based on the model.

Social impact

The social impact of the VAT rate increase is significant. The increase in the end-user price would result in an increase in household spending on natural gas. The average bill would increase from MDL 285 per month to MDL 313 per month, an increase of 9.7%. The compensation will reduce the share of the average bill, depending on the proposed scenario. The VAT compensation policy (*Scenario 1* and *2*) has a relatively limited impact on the share of natural gas costs in the disposable household income of vulnerable families. This is so because the compensation measure makes the situation of such families similar to what it would have been before the VAT increase.

If a lump-sum payment is chosen, the poorest families will enjoy a larger reduction in natural gas costs as a share of their disposable household income. Vulnerable families benefit most under *Scenario 3*, where compensation is calculated to keep the share of costs at a level that does not exceed 7.4% of their disposable household income. The results are presented in Table 5.14 and Figure 5.12.

Table 5.14. **Social impact of subsidy reform: percentage of natural gas costs in household disposable income under different scenarios, %**

Household income per capita	Scenario						
	Current price	No compensation	x% rule, VAT compensation in cash	x% rule, VAT compensa-tion with voucher	x% rule, compensation over x% in cash	MDL 4 000, lump sum in cash	MDL 4 000, VAT compensation with voucher
0-200	32.3%	35.5%	32.3%	32.3%	7.4%	29.2%	32.3%
200-400	18.5%	20.3%	18.2%	18.2%	6.0%	16.7%	18.2%
400-600	13.8%	15.2%	13.6%	13.6%	7.4%	12.8%	13.6%
600-800	11.5%	12.7%	11.4%	11.4%	7.4%	10.9%	11.4%
800-1 000	10.2%	11.1%	10.0%	10.0%	7.4%	9.7%	10.0%
1 000-1 200	9.2%	10.1%	9.1%	9.1%	7.4%	8.9%	9.1%
1 200-1 400	8.6%	9.4%	8.4%	8.4%	7.4%	8.4%	8.4%
1 400-1 600	8.1%	8.8%	8.0%	8.0%	7.4%	7.9%	7.9%
1 600-1 800	7.2%	7.8%	7.5%	7.5%	7.3%	7.8%	7.8%
1 800-2 000	6.6%	7.2%	7.0%	7.0%	7.2%	7.2%	7.2%
2 000-2 200	6.1%	6.7%	6.7%	6.7%	6.7%	6.7%	6.7%
2 200-2 400	5.8%	6.3%	6.3%	6.3%	6.3%	6.3%	6.3%
2 400-2 600	5.4%	6.0%	6.0%	6.0%	6.0%	6.0%	6.0%
2 600-2 800	5.2%	5.7%	5.7%	5.7%	5.7%	5.7%	5.7%
2 800-3 000	4.9%	5.4%	5.4%	5.4%	5.4%	5.4%	5.4%
3 000-	4.7%	5.2%	5.2%	5.2%	5.2%	5.2%	5.2%

Source: Authors' own calculations based on the model.

Figure 5.12. **Social impact of subsidy reform: percentage of natural gas expenditure in disposable household income under different scenarios, %**

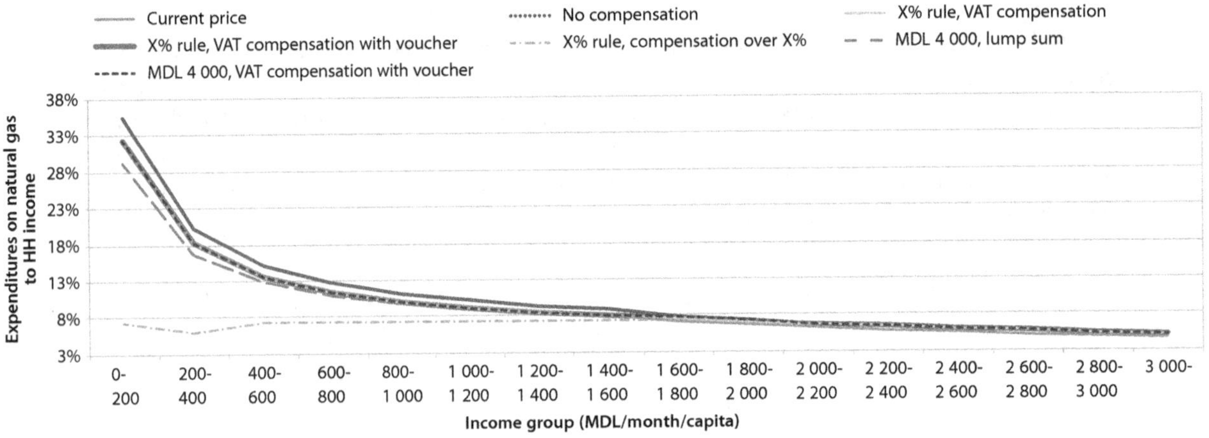

Source: Authors' own calculations based on the model

5.2.3. Heating

The model simulations show the impact of the increase of the VAT rate on end-user price for heating, heat energy consumption and GHG emissions level. The model results also provide some insights into the impact the VAT rate increase would have on the economy, the public budget and in terms of social effects.

Impact on end-user price

The gross average end-user price would increase from MDL 1.0234 to MDL 1.2281 per kWh. This is an increase of 20% over the current value.

Figure 5.13. **Impact of subsidy reform on end-user price for heating, in MDL**

Source: Authors' own calculations based on the model.

Impact on GHG emissions

The GHG emissions associated with the decrease in heat energy consumption would not be significant: 2 066 tonnes of CO_2 annually. If a compensation policy is introduced, the decrease will be about 600 tonnes of CO_2 annually, while in the case of compensation not only for VAT, but for all households that consume heat at a cost of more than 15% of disposable household income, the increase would be 224 tonnes of CO_2 annually, due to the increase of consumption by poorer households.

Table 5.15 and Figure 5.14 illustrate the impact on GHG emissions for all scenarios.

Table 5.15. **Impact of subsidy reform on the heating sector on GHG emissions under different scenarios, tCO_2 annually (VAT 20%)**

Scenario	No compensation	x% rule, VAT compensation in cash	x% rule, VAT compensation with voucher	x% rule, compensation over x% in cash	MDL 4 000, lump sum in cash	MDL 4 000, VAT compensation with voucher
CO_2 emissions from consumption at current price	93 063	93 063	93 063	93 063	93 063	93 063
CO_2 emissions from consumption at new price	90 997	90 997	90 997	90 997	90 997	90 997
CO_2 emissions from consumption at new price, with compensation	90 997	92 467	92 467	93 287	91 792	91 707
Decrease of CO_2 emissions	2 066	2 066	2 066	2 066	2 066	2 066
Decrease of CO_2 emissions, with compensation	2 066	596	596	-224	1 272	1 356

Source: Authors' own calculations based on the model.

Figure 5.14. **Impact of subsidy reform in the heating sector on GHG emissions under different scenarios, tCO_2 annually**

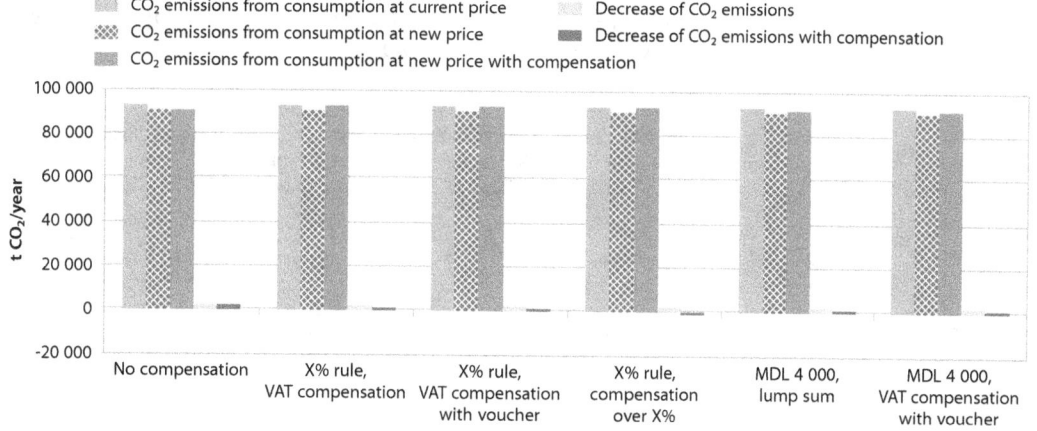

Source: Authors' own calculations based on the model.

Tables 5.16 and 5.17 present the impact of a reduced VAT increase on GHG emissions under all scenarios.

GHG emissions associated with the decrease in heat energy consumption would be: 826 tCO$_2$ annually if VAT is increased to 8% and 517 tCO$_2$ annually if VAT is increased to 5%. If a compensation policy is implemented, the decrease in case of a 8% VAT increase will be from 340 tCO$_2$ to 547 tCO$_2$ annually. In the case of compensation not only for VAT, but for all households that consume heat at a cost of more than 15% of disposable household income, the increase would be 734 tCO$_2$ annually due to the increase of consumption by poorer households. In case of a 5% VAT increase, the decrease of GHG emissions will be in the range of 213 tCO$_2$ to 342 tCO$_2$ annually, while in the case of compensation, not only for VAT, but for all households that consume heat at a cost of more than 15% of disposable household income, the increase would be 880 tCO$_2$ annually, due to the increase of consumption by poorer households. All these reductions do not represent a significant decrease of CO$_2$ emissions.

Table 5.16. **Impact of subsidy reform in the heating sector on GHG emissions under different scenarios, tCO$_2$ annually (VAT 8%)**

Scenario	No compensation	x% rule, VAT compensation in cash	x% rule, VAT compensation with voucher	x% rule, compensation over x% in cash	MDL 4 000, lump sum in cash	MDL 4 000, VAT compensation with voucher
CO$_2$ emissions from consumption at current price	93 063	93 063	93 063	93 063	93 063	93 063
CO$_2$ emissions from consumption at new price	92 237	92 237	92 237	92 237	92 237	92 237
CO$_2$ emissions from consumption at new price, with compensation	92 237	92 724	92 724	93 797	92 551	92 516
Decrease of CO$_2$ emissions	826	826	826	826	826	826
Decrease of CO$_2$ emissions, with compensation	826	340	340	-734	512	547

Source: Authors' own calculations based on the model.

Table 5.17. **Impact of subsidy reform in the heating sector on GHG emissions under different scenarios, tCO$_2$ annually (VAT 5%)**

Scenario	No compensation	x% rule, VAT compensation in cash	x% rule, VAT compensation with voucher	x% rule, compensation over x% in cash	MDL 4 000, lump sum in cash	MDL 4 000, VAT compensation with voucher
CO$_2$ emissions from consumption at current price	93 063	93 063	93 063	93 063	93 063	93 063
CO$_2$ emissions from consumption at new price	92 547	92 547	92 547	92 547	92 547	92 547
CO$_2$ emissions from consumption at new price, with compensation	92 547	92 850	92 850	93 944	92 743	92 721
Decrease of CO$_2$ emissions	517	517	517	517	517	517
Decrease of CO$_2$ emissions, with compensation	517	213	213	-880	320	342

Source: Authors' own calculations based on the model.

Impact on the public budget

The increase of the VAT rate on heat energy consumption would lead to an increase in budget revenue. The budget revenue would increase by MDL 480 million annually. The costs of the compensation would vary from MDL 166 million to MDL 553 million annually, depending on the compensation scenario. The administrative costs of distributing the compensation would be the highest in the case of cash compensation and would amount to MDL 45 million annually. For lump-sum cash distribution, the administrative costs would amount to MDL 11 million annually, while in the case of vouchers, they would amount to MDL 4 million annually.

In all cases but one, the budget surplus that will result from the VAT increase would be significant, from MDL 134 million to MDL 338 million. In one case (Scenario 3) the budget income will be lower than the budget expenditure. Table 5.18 and Figure 5.15 illustrate the impact on the budget under all scenarios.

Table 5.18. **Impact of subsidy reform in the heating sector on the public budget under different scenarios, in MDL annually (VAT 20%)**

Scenario	No compensation	x% rule, VAT compensation in cash	x% rule, VAT compensation with voucher	x% rule, compensation over x% in cash	MDL 4 000, lump sum in cash	MDL 4 000, VAT compensation with voucher
Budget income	480 863 350	533 443 560	533 443 560	562 772 520	509 276 999	506 261 545
Compensation costs	0	-353 391 635	-353 391 635	-553 171 605	-187 150 100	-166 249 357
Administration costs	0	-45 457 807	-3 788 151	-45 457 807	-11 289 260	-1 881 543
Budget surplus	480 863 350	134 594 117	176 263 774	-35 856 893	310 837 639	338 130 645

Source: Authors' own calculations based on the model.

Figure 5.15. **Impact of subsidy reform in the heating sector on the public budget: income, expenditure and surplus from the reform under different scenarios, in MDL**

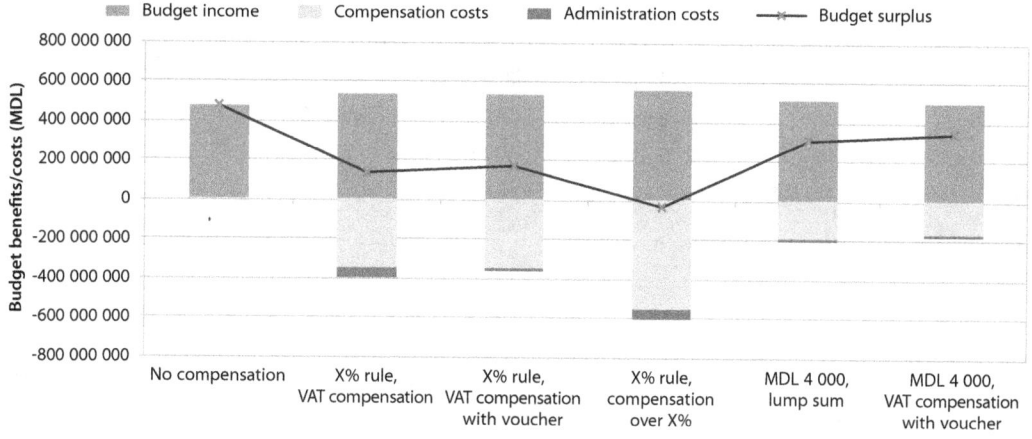

Source: Authors' own calculations based on the model.

Tables 5.19 and 5.20 present the impact of a reduced VAT increase on public budget in each scenario.

The budget revenue would increase by MDL 195 million annually in case of a 8% VAT increase and MDL 123 million annually in case of a 5% VAT increase. The costs of the compensation would vary from MDL 75 million to MDL 384 million annually, depending on the compensation scenario for a 8% VAT increase and MDL 41 million to MDL 346 million annually, depending on the compensation scenario for a 5% VAT increase.

The administrative costs of distributing the compensation would be the highest in the case of cash compensation and would amount to MDL 38 million annually. For lump-sum cash distribution, the administrative costs would amount to MDL 11 million annually, while in the case of vouchers, would amount to MDL 3 million annually.

In all cases but one, the budget surplus that will result from the VAT increase would be positive, from MDL 56 million to MDL 136 million in case of a 8% VAT increase and from MDL 21 million to MDL 85 million in case of a 5% VAT increase. In one case (Scenario 3), the budget income would be lower than budget expenditure.

Table 5.19. **Impact of subsidy reform in the heating sector on the public budget under different scenarios, in MDL annually (VAT 8%)**

Scenario	No compensation	x% rule, VAT compensation in cash	x% rule, VAT compensation with voucher	x% rule, compensation over x% in cash	MDL 4 000, lump sum in cash	MDL 4 000, VAT compensation with voucher
Budget income	195 301 085	210 964 995	210 964 995	245 528 817	205 421 028	204 297 536
Compensation costs	0	-116 760 603	-116 760 603	-384 437 870	-74 860 040	-66 215 113
Administration costs	0	-37 817 990	-3 151 499	-37 817 990	-11 289 260	-1 881 543
Budget surplus	195 301 085	56 386 403	91 052 893	-176 727 043	119 271 728	136 200 879

Source: Authors' own calculations based on the model.

Table 5.20. **Impact of subsidy reform in the heating sector on the public budget under different scenarios, in MDL annually (VAT 5%)**

Scenario	No compensation	x% rule, VAT compensation in cash	x% rule, VAT compensation with voucher	x% rule, compensation over x% in cash	MDL 4 000, lump sum in cash	MDL 4 000, VAT compensation with voucher
Budget income	122 525 013	132 014 820	132 014 820	166 235 650	128 659 131	127 975 827
Compensation costs	0	-72 969 722	-72 969 722	-345 909 237	-46 787 525	-41 370 337
Administration costs	0	-37 817 990	-3 151 499	-37 817 990	-11 289 260	-1 881 543
Budget surplus	122 525 013	21 227 108	55 893 599	-217 491 577	70 582 346	84 723 947

Source: Authors' own calculations based on the model.

Social impact

The social impact of the VAT rate increase is significant. The increase in the end-user price would result in an increase in household spending on heating. The average bill would increase from MDL 704 per month to MDL 826 per month. The share of the average bill in household income would increase from 19.1% to 22.4%. The compensation would decrease the share of the bill in disposable household income, depending on the proposed scenario. The VAT compensation (Scenarios 1 and 2) has a relatively limited impact on the share of heating costs in disposable household income for vulnerable families. This is so because the compensation package would make the situation of such families similar to what it would have been before the VAT increase.

In case of lump-sum payments, the poorest families would enjoy a higher decrease in the share of heat energy costs in their disposable income. Vulnerable families benefit most from Scenario 3, where compensation is calculated to keep the share of the costs at a level that does not exceed 15% of disposable household income. The results are presented in Table 5.21 and Figure 5.16.

Table 5.21. **Social impact of subsidy reform: percentage of expenditures on heating in disposable household income under different scenarios, % (VAT 20%)**

Household income per capita	Scenario						
	Current price	No compensation	x% rule, VAT compensation in cash	x% rule, VAT compensa-tion with voucher	x% rule, compensation over x% in cash	MDL 4 000, lump sum in cash	MDL 4 000, VAT compensation with voucher
0-200	76.5%	89.8%	76.5%	76.5%	15.0%	63.2%	76.5%
200-400	43.7%	51.3%	42.3%	42.3%	10.1%	36.0%	42.3%
400-600	32.8%	38.5%	31.8%	31.8%	11.8%	28.3%	31.8%
600-800	27.3%	32.1%	26.5%	26.5%	15.0%	24.4%	26.5%
800-1 000	24.0%	28.2%	23.3%	23.3%	15.0%	22.1%	23.3%
1 000-1 200	21.9%	25.7%	21.2%	21.2%	15.0%	20.6%	21.2%
1 200-1 400	20.3%	23.8%	19.7%	19.7%	15.0%	19.4%	19.7%
1 400-1 600	19.1%	22.4%	18.5%	18.5%	15.0%	18.6%	18.5%
1 600-1 800	17.0%	20.0%	16.5%	16.5%	15.0%	20.0%	20.0%
1 800-2 000	15.7%	18.4%	15.2%	15.2%	15.0%	18.4%	18.4%
2 000-2 200	14.6%	17.1%	14.6%	14.6%	15.0%	17.1%	17.1%
2 200-2 400	13.7%	16.1%	13.7%	13.7%	15.0%	16.1%	16.1%
2 400-2 600	12.9%	15.2%	12.9%	12.9%	15.0%	15.2%	15.2%
2 600-2 800	12.3%	14.4%	14.4%	14.4%	14.4%	14.4%	14.4%
2 800-3 000	11.7%	13.8%	13.8%	13.8%	13.8%	13.8%	13.8%
3 000-	11.2%	13.2%	13.2%	13.2%	13.2%	13.2%	13.2%

Source: Authors' own calculations based on the model.

Figure 5.16. **Social impact of subsidy reform: percentage of district heating expenditure in disposable household income under different scenarios, %**

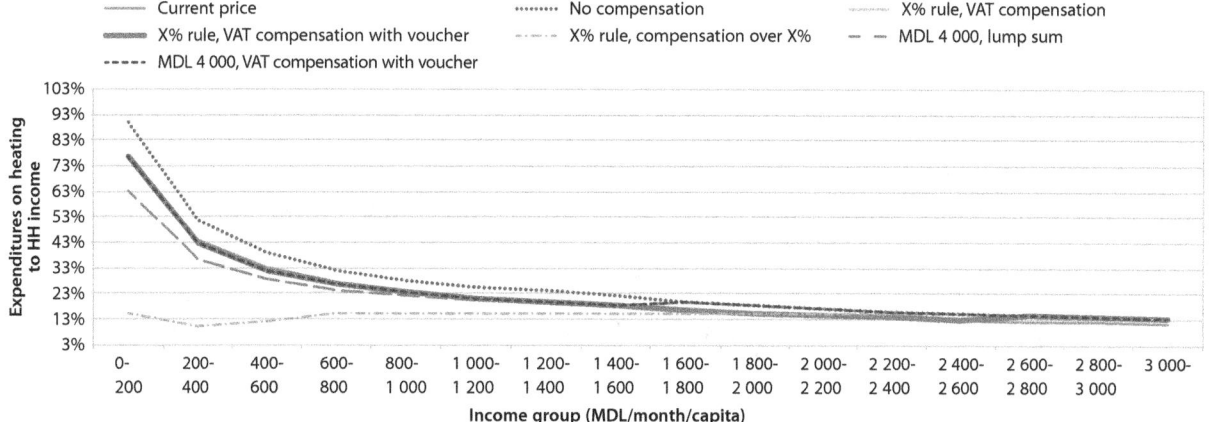

Source: Authors' own calculations based on the model.

Tables 5.22 and 5.23 present the impact of a reduced VAT increase on the percentage of electricity costs in disposable household income under different scenarios. This comparison is done for household income per capita of MDL 1 600 to 1 800 per month. As mentioned earlier, this range was chosen because it is the median income in Chisinau and Balti. The results are similar irrespective of the VAT increase (an increase of the share of heating costs in disposable household scenario of about 15% to 18%) except for the no-compensation scenario. This is so because the increase of the VAT is compensated for by the protection measures.

Table 5.22. **Social impact of subsidy reform: percentage of expenditures on heating in disposable household income under different scenarios, % (VAT 8%)**

Household income per capita	Scenario						
	Current price	No compensation	x% rule, VAT compensation in cash	x% rule, VAT compensa-tion with voucher	x% rule, compensation over x% in cash	MDL 4 000, lump sum in cash	MDL 4 000, VAT compensation with voucher
MDL 1 600-1 800	17.0%	18.2%	16.8%	16.8%	15.0%	18.2%	18.2%

Source: Authors' own calculations based on the model.

Table 5.23. **Social impact of subsidy reform: percentage of expenditures on heating in disposable household income under different scenarios, % (VAT 5%)**

Household income per capita	Scenario						
	Current price	No compensation	x% rule, VAT compensation in cash	x% rule, VAT compensa-tion with voucher	x% rule, compensation over x% in cash	MDL 4 000, lump sum in cash	MDL 4 000, VAT compensation with voucher
MDL 1 600-1 800	17.0%	17.8%	16.9%	16.9%	15.0%	17.8%	17.8%

Source: Authors' own calculations based on the model.

Comparative analysis of the results from the modelling is presented in the concluding chapter of the report. Major findings and conclusions are offered for further consideration by the government of Moldova.

Notes

1. The alternative would be to implement a simplified system that uses a proxy for an income-test (i.e. a number of employed persons in the household) and for energy consumption (energy consumption thresholds). In this case, the energy provider receives a set of conditions that allows for a VAT compensation. Then the energy provider issues a VAT exempted invoice and the responsible authority of the Ministry of Health, Labour and Social Protection performs a random verification. This is similar to the UK VAT compensation system.

2. Similarly to Scenario 2, a simplified system can be introduced. The energy provider receives a set of conditions that allows for a VAT compensation. These conditions could include a household situation (i.e. a number of employed persons in the household, which is a proxy for the MDL 4 000 poverty definition), or an issue of a certificate from the tax authority confirming the household's income below MDL 4 000. Then, the energy provider issues a VAT-exempted invoice.

3. Data for Spain was used as a proxy, as specified in Asche, F. et al. (2001).

References

Asche, F. et al. (2001), *Energy Taxes and Natural Gas Demand in EU-Countries*, CESifo Working Paper No. 516, Center for Economic Studies and Ifo Institute for Economic Research, Munich. www.cesifo-group.de/DocDL/cesifo_wp516.pdf.

Carbon Trust (2013), *Conversion Factors: Energy and Carbon Conversions 2013 Update*, Technical Report. Carbon Trust, London. https://www.carbontrust.com/resources/guides/carbon-footprinting-and-reporting/conversion-factors/.

DEFRA (2016), *Greenhouse Gas Reporting: Conversion Factors 2016*, UK Department for Environment, Food and Rural Affairs, London. https://www.gov.uk/government/publications/greenhouse-gas-reporting-conversion-factors-2016.

NBS (2017), *Household Income Distribution*, National Bureau of Statistics of Moldova, Chisinau. www.statistica.md/index.php?l=en. Accessed in September 2017.

Ruggeri Laderchi, C., A. Olivier and C. Trimble (2013), *Balancing Act: Cutting Energy Subsidies While Protecting Affordability*, Washington, DC: World Bank, doi: 10.1596/978-0-8213-9803-6 License: Creative Commons Attribution CC BY 3.0. https://openknowledge.worldbank.org/bitstream/handle/10986/12296/9780821397893.pdf;sequence=7.

Chapter 6

Conclusions and recommendations for Moldova

This chapter introduces the conclusions and recommendations that emerge from the current analysis. It proposes the best policy scenarios that can be further considered by the gov3ernment of the Republic of Moldova in moving forward with the energy subsidy reform in the country.

6.1. Major conclusions

Reforming energy subsidies in the Republic of Moldova by increasing the value added tax (VAT) rate to the standard 20% for electricity, natural gas and district heating energy will have significant budget revenue implications and socio-economic impacts. These impacts were also considered in the presence of five compensation measures that could be introduced to protect vulnerable households. These measures include:

- **Scenario 0:** No compensation for poor households
- **Scenario 1:** Income-tested (x% rule), VAT compensation in cash
- **Scenario 2:** Income-tested (x% rule), VAT compensation with voucher
- **Scenario 3:** Income-tested (x% rule), compensation in cash over y% of energy spending in disposable household income
- **Scenario 4:** MDL 4 000 poverty definition, lump sum
- **Scenario 5:** MDL 4 000 poverty definition, VAT compensation with voucher.

The analysis of the environmental impact of the reform, which was also considered in this study, especially for greenhouse (GHG) emissions, shows a limited impact compared to the current level of emissions from the sector. In fact, *Scenario 3* (compensation of costs in cash over x% of disposable household income) would even have a negative impact on GHG emissions, due to an increase in total energy consumption.

Experience shows that the easiest social protection measure to implement (administratively) is a voucher system that will compensate poor households for an increase of the VAT rate. This scenario has (almost) the lowest administrative costs. The level of administrative costs is an important factor, given the number of people who will need support if the reform is introduced. The study estimates that compensation measures will be needed to cover about 60% of households receiving services in the case of electricity, 60% in the case of natural gas, and even 70% in the case of heating. If household income increases in the future, the number of people needing support will drop.

Scenario 5 (arbitrary setting of income level that is entitled to compensation from the state) has similarly low administrative costs. This scenario is even easier to implement because it requires less administrative work on expenditure testing; yet, it may prove more difficult to implement from a social perspective, as spending on energy is not tested.

6.2. Selection of optimal social protection measures

Electricity sector

Table 6.1 presents a comparison and an overall assessment of the five main protection measures in the electricity sector, discussed in this report. These measures are assessed against six criteria:

- impact on the public budget (in monetary terms)
- impact on the public budget (in qualitative terms)
- ease of administering the protection measure
- level of protection provided by the measure to poor families
- linking the social protection measure to energy consumption
- incentive to implement energy efficiency (EE) measures.

Each criterion is assessed by a simple + and − sign, which stand for a positive and negative impact, respectively. A single sign stands for low impact, two signs show a medium impact, and three signs high impact. The signs are then summed up and show the overall assessment.

This overall multi-criteria assessment shows that the income-tested, VAT compensation with voucher" is the most advisable to implement, followed by the MDL 4 000 poverty definition, VAT compensation with voucher policy. The MDL 4 000 poverty definition, lump-sum compensation measure has certain advantages, the most promising of which is that the lump sum can be used as an incentive to stimulate energy-efficiency measures. On the other hand, this scenario will have a small impact on the public budget, because public funds will be overspent on protection measures (MDL 177 million as compared with MDL 255 million for the income-tested, VAT compensation with voucher scenario).

A VAT increase for electricity would be the easiest to implement. Relatively low consumption will have a small impact on household income; compensation would thus be relatively inexpensive. The budget surplus from this measure is not the most significant (about MDL 255 million annually), but given the other criteria, this scenario is preferable.

Table 6.1. **Comparative assessment of social protection scenarios in the electricity sector**

Scenario	No compensation	Income-tested, VAT compensation in cash	Income-tested, VAT compensation with voucher	Income-tested, compensation over 6% in cash	MDL 4 000 poverty definition, lump-sum compensation in cash	MDL 4 000 poverty definition, VAT compensation with voucher
Impact on public budget (MDL)	545 699 462	112 119 902	254 861 200	-54 482 185	176 784 930	283 396 347
Impact on public budget (qualitative)	+++	+	++	-	+	++
Ease of administering the measure	+++	-	++	-	+	++
Level of protection provided by the measure to poor families	---	++	++	+++	++	++
Link of social protection measure to energy consumption	---	+	+	++	-	-
Incentive to implement energy efficiency measures	+	-	-	-	+	-
Overall assessment	-/+	+++	++++++	+++	++++	+++++

Note: + = positive impact; − = negative impact.

As for the choice of the VAT rate (20% or reduced), Table 6.2 provides an assessment of how the three rates analysed (5%, 8% and 20%) compare with the main assessment criteria.

The 20% VAT generates the highest budget surplus and impact on CO_2 emissions. However, the compensation costs (social transfers) for this rate are the highest: almost three times higher than for the 8% VAT rate and more than four times higher than for the 5% VAT rate. In result, the share of electricity costs in disposable household income for a median group (with an income of MDL 1 600 to MDL 1 800 per month per capita) is slightly lower than the share of costs under both the 8% and 5% VAT rate. These cost shares are similar for lower household incomes, while the opposite is observed in the case of high-income families.

Administrative costs are only slightly higher for the 20% VAT rate, because the compensation for an 8% or 5% VAT will cover a similar number of families (slightly higher in case of 20%) while unit compensation amounts will be lower, which, globally, does not change the administrative costs.

Table 6.2. **Comparative assessment of VAT rate**

VAT rate	20%	8%	5%
Budget revenue (MDL annually)	594 232 440	236 949 633	148 524 297
Compensation costs (MDL annually)	-326 394 759	-114 757 473	-72 600 738
Administration costs (MDL annually)	-12 976 482	-11 527 508	-11 527 508
Budget surplus (MDL annually)	254 861 200	110 664 652	64 396 051
Decrease in CO_2 emissions, with compensation (tCO_2 annually)	497	232	142
Share of electricity costs in disposable household income for income of MDL 1 600 to MDL 1 800 per month per capita (%)	5.3%	5.7%	5.5%

Source: The model.

Natural gas sector

Our analysis shows that it would be more difficult to implement an increase of the VAT rate on natural gas. A significant part of natural gas is used for heating, and for those households, the share of natural gas costs in disposable household income is significant. The budget surplus from the second scenario (income-tested, VAT compensation with voucher) of about MDL 121 million could and, ideally, should, however, be earmarked for energy-efficiency programmes for residential buildings that reduce energy consumption for heating.

As noted earlier, the MDL 4 000 poverty definition, lump-sum compensation has many advantages, including using the lump sum as an incentive for implementing energy-efficiency measures. This, however, is not definitive, because there is no guarantee that households will use the lump sum for this purpose. The first major challenge is that energy-efficiency measures are difficult to implement on an apartment level in multi-apartment blocks. People living in such buildings in Moldova do not always make a collaborative effort to improve energy efficiency in their blocks. Introducing energy-efficiency programmes for residential buildings could be a more efficient way of spending the budget surplus. The second challenge is that households may switch to using other energy carriers instead of making energy-efficiency investments. In the case of houses, people can use wood or coal while at the same time receiving compensation for a VAT increase in natural gas.

As with electricity, Table 6.3 provides a simple assessment of the proposed scenarios in the natural gas sector. The overall result from this assessment is comparable to the assessment of the electricity sector. The **best policy is to implement the income-tested, VAT compensation with voucher,** followed by the MDL 4 000, poverty definition, VAT compensation with voucher measure.

Table 6.3. **Comparative assessment of social protection scenarios in the natural gas sector**

Scenario	No compensation	Income-tested, VAT compensation in cash	Income-tested, VAT compensation with voucher	Income-tested, compensation over 10% in cash	MDL 4 000 poverty definition, lump-sum compensation in cash	MDL 4 000, poverty definition, VAT compensation with voucher
Impact on public budget (MDL)	222 107 322	63 363 051	121 347 067	-104 120 512	90 007 495	131 054 185
Impact on public budget (qualitative)	+++	+	++	-	+	++
Ease of administering the measure	+++	-	++	-	+	++
Level of protection provided by the measure to poor families	---	++	++	+++	++	++
Link of social protection measure to energy consumption	---	+	+	++	-	-
Incentive to implement EE measures	+	-	-	-	+	-
Overall assessment	-/+	+++	++++++	+++	++++	+++++

Note: + - positive impact; - negative impact.

Heating sector

The most difficult policy to implement is a VAT increase for heating. The costs of heat energy are already very high: twice as much as for energy from natural gas. At the same time, it is more difficult for end users to control their heat energy costs when heat is provided by the district heating system. Increasing the district heating price would thus make consumers first consider disconnecting from the district heating network and not undertaking energy-efficiency measures. This would lead to an increase in the unit costs of heat and electrical energy, whose production is linked to heating. It is thus recommended that the implementation of a VAT increase for heating be postponed until disposable household income increases. After such an increase occurs, a smaller number of people living in Chisinau and Balti will need social support.

However, if a decision is made to increase the VAT for heating, it is best to implement this policy in parallel with a social and/or energy-efficiency programme. Thus, Scenario 3 (compensation for all families that spend more than 15% of their household income on heat energy) is worth noting, even if it has a negative impact on the national budget. Scenario 2 (VAT increase compensation by voucher) can be introduced if the budget surplus is used to support energy-efficiency programmes for residential buildings in the Chisinau and Balti.

The analysis shows that this reform is worth pursuing, and the recommended policy is the one suggested under Scenario 2. The reform is also socially justifiable, as it is still better to protect poor households rather than all households, including those that are well-off.

6.3. Main recommendations

The analysis in this study shows that it is worth reforming the VAT-related energy subsidies in Moldova, because the reform can yield significant budget revenue and a reduction (albeit modest) of GHG emissions. However, given the significant impact of the VAT increase on consumer end-price and the related household spending on energy, the reform should not be introduced before a robust system of social protection measures is instituted.

The analysis shows that reforms are the easiest to implement in the electricity sector, followed by reforms in the natural gas sector. At this stage, increasing the VAT rate on heat is not desirable, as prices in this sector are already high in Moldova and the social impact will be significant. It would thus be preferable to postpone reforms in the heating sector until household incomes increase.

In sum, the optimal social protection measures identified in this analysis to ensure energy affordability for poor households are:

- In the electricity sector: income-tested, VAT compensation with voucher, followed by MDL 4 000 poverty definition, VAT compensation with voucher policy;

- In the natural gas sector: income-tested, VAT compensation with voucher followed by the MDL 4 000, poverty definition, VAT compensation with voucher measure.

To put these reform measures into effect, Moldova will need to do more work to translate this current analysis into legislative proposals. Any new fiscal policy package should include, among other things, a clear definition of the low-income households that will be targeted and a carefully designed and resourced system of support delivery.

ORGANISATION FOR ECONOMIC CO-OPERATION AND DEVELOPMENT

The OECD is a unique forum where governments work together to address the economic, social and environmental challenges of globalisation. The OECD is also at the forefront of efforts to understand and to help governments respond to new developments and concerns, such as corporate governance, the information economy and the challenges of an ageing population. The Organisation provides a setting where governments can compare policy experiences, seek answers to common problems, identify good practice and work to co-ordinate domestic and international policies.

The OECD member countries are: Australia, Austria, Belgium, Canada, Chile, the Czech Republic, Denmark, Estonia, Finland, France, Germany, Greece, Hungary, Iceland, Ireland, Israel, Italy, Japan, Korea, Latvia, Lithuania, Luxembourg, Mexico, the Netherlands, New Zealand, Norway, Poland, Portugal, the Slovak Republic, Slovenia, Spain, Sweden, Switzerland, Turkey, the United Kingdom and the United States. The European Union takes part in the work of the OECD.

OECD Publishing disseminates widely the results of the Organisation's statistics gathering and research on economic, social and environmental issues, as well as the conventions, guidelines and standards agreed by its members.

www.ingramcontent.com/pod-product-compliance
Lightning Source LLC
Chambersburg PA
CBHW082353220526
45470CB00008B/2729